DIMENSIONS OF
AUTHORITY IN THE
RELIGIOUS LIFE

Joseph H. Fichter, S.J.   Charles J. Corcoran, C.S.C.

Louis J. Putz, C.S.C.   Mother Rose Elizabeth, C.S.C.

72262

BX
4212
: T47

L Theological Institute for Local Superiors

UNIVERSITY OF NOTRE DAME PRESS • 1966

Imprimi Potest: Howard J. Kenna, C.S.C., Provincial

Nihil Obstat: Joseph Hoffman, C.S.C., Censor Deputatus

Imprimatur: ✠ Leo A. Pursley, D.D.,
          Bishop of Fort Wayne-South Bend

UNIVERSITY OF NOTRE DAME PRESS
NOTRE DAME — LONDON

Copyright © 1966 by
University of Notre Dame Press
Notre Dame, Indiana

Library of Congress Catalog Card Number: 66-14632

Manufactured in the United States of America

These articles were published previously in the Proceedings of the Sisters' Institute of Spirituality 1958 and 1959, copyrighted by the University of Notre Dame Press.

PREFACE

Each year since 1953 the Department of Theology of the University of Notre Dame has sponsored an institute for local superiors, with the encouragement of the Sacred Congregation for Religious and the cooperation of the Conference of Major Superiors of Women and the Sister Formation Conference.

The aim of the Theological Institute for Local Superiors, formerly known as the Institute of Spirituality, is to assist those committed to the direction of the spiritual and apostolic life of their communities in developing a profound vision and sense of mission in their work for the Church.

The publication each year of the proceedings of these institutes has greatly aided superiors in transmitting to their subjects the insights gained at the meetings. And, judging by the response, of equal value have been the volumes in the Religious Life in the Modern World series. Each of these, devoted to a particular aspect of the life of religious today, consists of selections from *Proceedings* of various years.

Following the suggestions of Reverend Charles Corcoran, C.S.C., the editors have compiled this fifth volume in the series, *Dimensions of Authority in the Religious Life,* with the hope that it will further the work of the Institute in bringing increased vitality and meaning to the life of all women religious.

ALBERT L. SCHLITZER, C.S.C.
General Chairman, Theological
Institute for Local Superiors

CONTENTS

THE SOCIOLOGICAL ASPECTS

OF

THE ROLE OF AUTHORITY IN THE ADAPTATION OF THE RELIGIOUS COMMUNITY FOR THE APOSTOLATE

Reverend Joseph H. Fichter, S.J.

Introduction

The intrusion of sociological analysis into the sacred precincts of the religious community may seem a strange and disturbing approach where hitherto only the canon lawyer and the ascetical theologian have been completely at home. In this whole discussion there are assumptions that the social scientist must accept without question and there are areas where he does not dare to tread. The presence and operation of divine grace, the intentions and internal virtues of the people under consideration, the degree of personal merit involved in their actions — these are all aspects of religious life that the social scientist does not scrutinize. This does not mean, however, that nothing else remains as a field of analysis open to the sociologist.

The problem under discussion is one that plagues large social organizations everywhere in our dynamic and complex American society. How can the function of management be improved so that the production of the organization can be increased? As in other areas of human relations, we are here confronted with people in an organized system performing functions under direction. How can these people be directed efficiently and effectively? In other words, how can authority be employed so that more and better efforts are expended to get more and better results? This may seem a bald and profane way to talk about a

1

religious community, with its dedicated functionaries and supernatural goals, but it may also serve as a realistic and refreshing approach.

There are more than a quarter-million Americans who have dedicated themselves to the full-time service of the Catholic Church, and the great majority of these are in religious communities of various kinds. It is probably safe to say that the original talent of these people is not of a lower order than that found among the personnel of scientific, professional, business, political and other American organizations. Nor can we say — on the basis of any empirical research done up to this time — that the religious system has not been in its own way as successful and productive as these other social systems in America. No one has seriously attempted to formulate usable norms of measurement that are transposable among these various systems, although there seems to be general agreement that American scientific, as well as business, pursuits have been highly successful.

Nevertheless, since religious communities are composed of and directed by fallible human beings, and since religious functionaries are perfectible human instruments, there can be no doubt that apostolic performance, as well as the organization and training of these people, are open to improvement. We all know of individuals in the service of the Church who do not put forth constant full effort, of others whose talents and energies seem to have been left largely untapped, and even of others who have defected from their status. Human failures are no new experience — even in the Church of Christ. These people always receive our prayers and our sympathy, but most often they are looked upon as personal and individual delinquents whose inadequacies stem exclusively from weakness and lack of virtue.

Social scientists have provided considerable empirical data to demonstrate that personal and psychological factors are only partial explanations of human behavior. The social system in which a man operates, the cultural pressures that surround him, the manner in which his colleagues — and above all, his superiors — deal with him; these are also significant factors that have an effect upon his patterns of behavior. These environmental elements are the material in which the social scientist works. Sociological research has turned up some fruitful analyses of personnel administration, organizational forms, training programs, performance of roles. It seems probable that similar research among religious groups can attain equally fruitful results.

These sociological studies of various secular groups provide a source of knowledge and comparison for our present discussion. Generalizations drawn from them give us notions about what works and what does not work in social relations and structures; but they cannot be applied in every detail to religious personnel and groups. The fact is that religious organizations exhibit certain peculiar characteristics that must be studied separately. In some important respects the goals and values that act as cultural criteria in the judgment of operations in religious communities differ from those found in secular groupings. For this reason we must turn to another source of data.

It is therefore scientifically legitimate, and even necessary, that we study the purposes, goals and values of religious communities, as these are expressed in the recommendations of the Holy Father, the prescriptions of Canon Law, the Institutes of religious communities, and in the observations made by various commentators on all of these. Such data are social facts, not only because they influence the conduct of the people involved, but also because they tell us what these groups are supposed to be doing. They provide a knowledge of the norms, standards and expectations, against which the observer may measure the actual operation of the religious community as a social organization.

It must be clearly understood that the present study is a specialized sociological investigation of the relationship between authority and apostolic efficiency in the religious community. We are not directly concerned with the practice of obedience by the religious subject, but with the exercise of authority by the religious superior. Similarly, although personal sanctification is clearly an end of the organized religious life, and although inner sanctity is both personal and social, our attention is focused mainly on the external apostolic functions and purposes of the group. Briefly stated, then, the question is this: how do leaders get productive results from their followers?[1]

In order to get at the answer to our question, the pivotal areas of research are *authority, community* and *apostolate*. In sociological terminology these are the areas of administration, structure and function, and in the language of the commercial and business world they may be translated as management, organization and production. These terms symbolize a kind of triad, with influences running back and forth among them, but with effective production or service in the apostolate as the continuing goal, and with the exercise of authority and the mode of organization as means or instruments to the goal.

---

1. Since the second World War, the term "manpower management" has come into wide usage. "It is charged with providing leadership and guidance in the employment of manpower, society's most distinctive, versatile, complicated and valuable resource." Dale Yoder, *Personnel Principles and Policies,* (New York: Prentice-Hall, 1952), p. 12.

I

Aspects of Religious Authority

Authority is the correlative of obedience, and like obedience it may be analyzed from various points of view. The canonical and theological aspects of both authority and obedience in the religious sphere have been explored.[1] Comparatively little has been done, however, from the sociological point of view. In this context, then, authority refers to the leadership of the religious group, and is roughly synonymous with management and administration in the secular group. Since authority is so closely intertwined with obedience, it is practically impossible to deal with the leader without reference to the follower. The focus of attention here, however, will be mainly on the former and only incidentally on the latter.

The common sociological approach is to look upon authority as both a social status and a social role. Leadership *is* something and leadership *does* something. Here again, the two concepts of status and role are so intertwined that great care is required to analyze them separately. The classic formula of Ralph Linton has been refined by other social scientists, so that we now think of a person's status as that which he *is* in relation to other people, and the role as that which he *does*, the functional pursuit of goals.[2]

Leadership is therefore expressed in both status and role. It may be looked at both as a positional and as a functional phenomenon. In a most general sense the individual who has the most prestige also enjoys the most social power, even when he is not in an "official" position. In the concrete order, of course, it is always a person who has the status

---

1. Karl Rahner, "Eine ignatianische Grundhaltung," *Stimmen der Zeit,* vol. 158, (1955-56), pp. 253-267, points out that during the decade after the war, in Middle Europe alone, at least fifty books and articles have been devoted to this theme. Translated as "A Basic Ignatian Concept," *Woodstock Letters,* vol. 86, no. 4, (November, 1957), pp. 291-310.

2. Ralph Linton, *The Study of Man,* (New York: Appleton-Century, 1936), chapter 8; John W. Bennett and Melvin M. Tumin, *Social Life, Structure and Function,* (New York: Knopf, 1948), chapters 6 and 7; Joseph H. Fichter, *Sociology,* (Chicago: University of Chicago Press, 1957), chapters 2 and 9.

of leadership and who enacts the role of leadership. Like status and role, person and position are inextricably interwoven.[3]

POSITIONAL LEADERSHIP

Positional authority or leadership refers to the office, status or position which the person occupies. This position of authority may be acquired in various ways. It may be *inherited,* as an office of nobility or royalty. It may be *assumed,* as when a person simply "takes over" the authority either by illegally usurping it or because of the default of others. Leadership may be *elective,* as when the subjects or their representatives vote for the leader; or finally, it may be appointive, as when a higher authority selects others to fill minor roles.[4]

The essence of positional leadership is that the incumbent is able to exert authority by virtue of the office or status he possesses. It is the authority attached to the office that transfers to the person, quite aside from his personal intelligence, virtue or other talents. In religious communities this office is neither inherited nor assumed. It may, however, be either elective or appointive. The point of distinction here is that the position itself is a value; it is superior to other relative positions in the social structure, and it is handed over by others to whom the person in authority may be personally inferior.[5]

In religious communities, as in every other organization, positional leadership is shared and graded. There is never a single total leader in the sense that only one office exists. This is true even in the most authoritarian political systems. For example, a distinction of positional leadership can always be derived from the general functions to be per-

---

3. For a concise sociological approach to definitions in this area of analysis, see Herbert Goldhamer and Edward Shils, "Types of Power and Status," *The American Journal of Sociology,* vol. 45, no. 2, (September, 1939), pp. 171-182. See also Chester I. Bernard, *Organization and Management,* (Cambridge: Harvard University Press, 1952), chap. 4, "The Nature of Leadership."

4. From the point of view of the subject, legitimate power, as distinguished from coercion, may be legal, traditional or charismatic. *Ibid.,* p. 171.

5. At this point we may omit the peculiar theory attributed to Fr. Delos, O.P., who remarks that "in a society authority does not render one man subject to another; it is not an individual that an individual obeys; ultimately he obeys only a parent-idea which marks a purpose, and sets forth a good. There is no subjection of man to man but a co-ordination of acts, and a differentiation of functions toward the common good. There is no need to insist on the importance of this notion of social authority; it provides an extremely noble and fertile conception of authority and of obedience." Quoted by Abbé Kothen, "The Superior, Servant of the Common Good," in Albert Plé (ed.) *Religious Sisters,* (Westminster, Newman Press, 1954), p. 139. If this means nothing more than the obedience demanded by the social function itself, we shall discuss it below when considering the Apostolate.

formed. This distinction is taken from military terminology and has been applied in other forms of organization. The *staff* officers are the planners and the policy makers; they are top management in the organization. The *line* officers are those who direct the immediate operations, who "get out" the production, who see to it that the members of the organization perform their assigned functions.[6]

The gradation of leadership and the hierarchy of office may be demonstrated in religious communities of women. "In the stricter sense those only are to be considered superioresses who *from their office* have a stable authority over the institute as a whole, over a province, or over a house. By name they are most frequently called the superioress general, the provincial and the local superioress. One exception to this rule is the office of visitatrix, which in some communities commits permanent authority." [7]

An important aspect of religious authority that distinguishes it from every other type of authority is its *sacred* character. A peculiarly exalted status is ascribed to the office itself because the superior holds the place of God in reference to the subjects. Whether or not the person acts in a godlike manner, a sacred and charismatic nimbus surrounds the office that he holds. From this point of view, it is the office of authority itself, rather than the personal qualities of the officer, that provides the right to command and the reason for obeying. As Ignatius Loyola wrote, "the superior is not to be obeyed because he is prudent, or kind, or divinely gifted in any other way, but for the sole reason that he holds the place of God and exercises the authority of Him who says, 'He who hears you hears me, and he who despises you despises me'." [8]

PERSONAL LEADERSHIP

Personal leadership is that which is exercised by virtue of the qualities or competences through which the official person is enabled to fulfill the functions contained in the leadership role. These qualities do not

---

6. See Douglas McGregor, "The Staff Function in Human Relations," *Journal of Social Issues,* vol. 4, no. 3, (Summer, 1948), pp. 6-23; also L. Urwick, "The Personnel Manager is a Staff Officer," in *Personnel Management in Relation to Factory Organization,* (London: Institute of Labour Management, 1943), pp. 16-20, 23-27.

7. Thomas J. Bowe, *Religious Superioresses, A Historical Synopsis and a Commentary,* (Washington: Catholic University Press, 1946), pp. 43-44. Italics added.

8. William Young, *St. Ignatius' Own Story,* (Chicago: Regnery, 1956), "Letter On Obedience," p. 111.

"give" or "contain" authority in the sense that the office itself does. Hence, just as it is possible that a person who holds the position of authority may not have the qualities of leadership, so also is it possible that persons who possess the qualities of leadership do not hold the position of leader.

The most general types of personal leadership may be roughly categorized as the managerial, the expert and the charismatic. It is probably seldom that all three types are fully realized simultaneously in the same person, but it seems true to say that some degree of each is found in the most successful leader. The *charismatic* quality is found in the person who is imbued with special charm and grace and has powers of arousing deep loyalty and devotion among his followers. He has an exciting personality, is recognized by others as a "natural" leader, and appears to have an inner compulsion and dedication to the cause for which he works.[9]

The concept of charisma appears to be particularly applicable to religious leaders although it also fits well the great national and military leaders. We are speaking here only of personal charisma although Weber referred also to the charisma of office. "The personal charisma is probably the original one, but official charisma has gained tremendous importance in the history of religious groups. No doubt, there is something elementary and irresistible in personal charisma, in contrast to which official charisma appears less efficacious. The latter may be more clearly defined than the vague, often indescribable, personal type, but it is narrower, shallower, and more limited. There is an additional important difference. Charisma of personal character appeals more to the emotions; official charisma is more 'rational.' Whereas the former claims complete loyalty, even personal surrender, the latter usually demands a circumscribed or 'tempered' obedience."[10]

The quality of *expertness* that characterizes some leaders seems to be particularly appreciated by Americans. This refers to the fact that a person has special skill and knowledge through which he becomes known as an "authority" in his own field of endeavor. Sometimes the expert leader stands behind the active and official leader and provides the "brains" for certain segments of the total operation. Sometimes an ex-

---

9. Max Weber: *The Theory of Social and Economic Organization,* tr. A. M. Henderson and Talcott Parsons, (New York: Oxford University Press, 1947), "Charismatic Authority," pp. 358-363.

10. Joachim Wach, *Sociology of Religion,* (Chicago: University of Chicago Press, 1944), p. 337.

pert leader oversteps the limits of his expertness and because of his prestige is influential in fields of which he knows practically nothing.[11]

There are expert leaders of all kinds in the religious communities of America and some of them become official superiors and superioresses. The more that the religious communities involve themselves in the apostolic functions of education, research, hospital work, social ,work and others, and the more they follow the Pope's injunction that their functionaries must be as well trained as similar people in the lay society, the greater will be the increase in numbers of expert leaders. This appears to be a necessary accommodation to the American appreciation for, and need for, specialized skills and knowledge.

The third type of authority that demands personal qualifications may be called *managerial* or executive leadership. This refers to the fact that the individual has the ability to lead and direct other persons to the common end. Chester Barnard remarks that "executive work is not that *of* the organization, but the specialized work of *maintaining* the organization in operation." [12] This appears to be a relatively scarce ability in the American system where it is so desperately needed because of our increasingly complex and specialized organization, and it is the type that commands the highest salaries in the occupational system. A person of high managerial competency is theoretically able to perform his function regardless of the type and purpose of the organization in which he operates.

This managerial function, prescinding from the type of apostolic work done by the religious community, seems to be the focus of attention in some writings on the religious superior. In other words, the maintenance of the organization in operation is the managerial function. "The religious government consists in the conducting of a religious community towards its end. The end of this religious government is to

---

11. Albert Einstein and Henry Ford are typical examples of experts who sometimes made "authoritative" statements far beyond their ken. Parsons shows clearly that the professional's exercise of authority is legitimate only when it is based on his superior technical competence. Talcott Parsons, *Essays in Sociological Theory,* revised edition, (Glencoe: Free Press, 1954), "The Professions and Social Structure," pp. 34-49.

12. See Chester I. Barnard, *The Functions of the Executive,* (Cambridge: Harvard University Press, 1945), chapter 15, "The Executive Functions," p. 215. Joseph F. Gallen, S.J., "Renovation and Adaptation," *Review For Religious,* vol. 14, (November, 1955), p. 309, gives us a salutary caution at this point. "Superiors who are mere executives, financiers, expert in public relations, good managers, skilled directors of external works, and those who have lost familiarity with spiritual principles or are spiritually illiterate have already failed in their first essential duty."

create a favorable 'milieu' for the acquisition of perfection, by insuring the observance of the Institute's Constitutions and by fostering a good spirit in the community. Secondly, the end of the religious government is to stimulate the fervor of each of its members in tending to perfection. . . . The superior's part is, first, to govern her community, secondly to perfect the personal formation of her subjects." [13]

TRAITS OF LEADERSHIP

A multitude of studies have been made in attempting to isolate and analyze the personal qualities or characteristics of the successful leader. Out of these impressionistic analyses it was hoped that certain universal traits of leadership could be identified. Bogardus proposed five general qualities: imagination, foresight, flexibility, versatility and inhibition.[14] Munson suggested the following: personality, manner, use of language, tact, cheerfulness, courtesy, justice and discipline.[15] Bird investigated and compared about twenty previously made lists of leadership traits and found that they contained altogether seventy-nine different items which were supposed to characterize leadership.[16]

Empirical studies of lay leadership in the sociology of religion are perhaps more realistic than these lists of generalized traits in that they reflect the opinions of those most involved in the situation. The best we can say for these studies is that they are focused on the religious group itself and that they indicate what the people think they want in a typical Catholic leader. Even here one finds little more than the most general traits like religious knowledge, courtesy, unselfishness, honesty, willingness to work, enthusiasm, ability to express thoughts, organizational ability.[17]

When we search the literature on religious superiors we find again a list of general personal qualities which the good leader is supposed to

---

13. See *Proceedings* of the 1953 Sisters' Institute of Spirituality, edited by Joseph E. Haley, (Notre Dame: University of Notre Dame Press, 1954); Paul Philippe: "The Formation of Novices and the Government of Communities," p. 17.

14. E. S. Bogardus, *Fundamentals of Social Psychology*, (New York: Appleton, 1942), chapter 12.

15. Edward L. Munson, *The Management of Men*, (New York: Holt, 1921).

16. Charles Bird, *Social Psychology*, (New York: Appleton-Century, 1940). See also Bertrand Russell, *Power, A New Social Analysis*, (New York: Norton, 1938), and especially Alvin W. Gouldner (ed.), *Studies in Leadership*, (New York: Harper, 1950), pp. 21-25.

17. See this list in the author's *Social Relations in the Urban Parish*, (Chicago: University of Chicago Press, 1954), chapter 3, "Nuclear Parishioners and Leaders;" also *Soziologie der Pfarrgruppen*, (Muenster: Aschendorff, 1958), chapter 5, "Laienkraefte in der Gruppenfuehrung."

possess. One superior said briefly: "In our office we shall practice the essential virtues of the leader: fortitude, prudence and justice," and then described each of these qualities.[18] Elsewhere we read that "the one to be chosen for the office of superioress should be outstanding in character and ability. Her qualities should be those of humility, piety, firmness, seriousness in the observance of discipline, patience, charity, knowledge, prudence, affability, justice, and good example."[19] Still another list of the "qualities necessary for the superior" repeats most of these traits, but adds an aside from Thomas Aquinas to the effect that a "holy soul who has no sense of governing" should not be chosen in preference to a good administrator who is less advanced in holiness.[20]

It is probable that the "situational approach," as indicated under the various aspects of religious authority discussed below, will help to evolve a more realistic concept of leadership than these lists of descriptive qualities. It may provide an insight, however, to suggest that the traits desired by the local superior in the subjects newly entering his community may likewise be the qualities desired by the subject in his superior.

The type of persons welcome to the community are: (a) Humble, unpretentious persons who let themselves be told a few things and do not think that they know everything better than anyone else. (b) Persons who do not mind sacrifice and are not afraid of a bit of rough going, who are not timorous, hesitant weaklings. (c) Persons who are willing to pitch right in and are not always giving work a wide berth. (d) Persons who are competent to do the job they are supposed to do. (e) Persons who have a spirit of mortification and are willing to carry on in the patient endurance of what simply has to be borne. (f) In a word, persons who can take whatever is demanded of them as regards climate, occupation, primitive housing conditions, poor or distasteful food, and such like hurdles.[21]

In the last analysis, the "traits" of leadership refer to the personal

---

18. Marie-Therese Lemerle, O.S.U., "The Superior, Servant of the Common Good," in Albert Plé, O.P. (ed.) *Communal Life,* (Westminster: Newman Press, 1957), p. 294.

19. Thomas Bowe, *op. cit.,* p. 68, with references to Guidus Cocchi, *Commentarium in Codicem Iuris Canonici ad Usum Scholarum,* (Taurinorum Augustae, Marietti, 1939), vol. 4, p. 53, n. 24.

20. Paul Philippe, O.P., *op. cit.,* p. 18, with reference to Thomas Aquinas, *Summa Theologica* II-II, q. 185, art. 3; where he says that "nothing hinders one from being more fitted for the office of governing, who does not excel in the grace of holiness"; and *Questiones Quodlibetales,* 8, art. 6, "it is possible that a person who is holier may lack that which is needed in authority, like knowledge, industry and influence, which a less holy person may possess."

21. This list of qualifications is presented by Winfrid Herbst, S.D.S., "Thoughts on Transfers," *Review for Religious,* vol. xv, (July, 1956), pp. 202-

qualifications of the individual who is in the superior office. In the contemporary religious community we may presume that the difference in these qualifications between the superior and the subject is not as great as the difference in the difficulty of the function to be performed by both. We may often expect, therefore, that difficult and important functions of leadership will be more poorly performed than the lesser functions of followers. As Rahner says, "the defective fulfillment of higher obligations cruelly lays bare the shortcomings of a man's capacities which previously escaped our attention." [22]

These observations concerning talent and performance have significant implications for the person who exercises authority in religious communities. "Superiors should not act as if by nature or by reason of their office they are more intelligent, more clever persons, more morally steadfast, more provident and wise in the ways of the world. This may be true in individual cases, for the world is not so constructed that only the more stupid become superiors. But it should be soberly stated (for subjects, lest they demand too much of superiors, something which would be unjust and show a lack of charity; for superiors, lest they delude themselves) : the higher the office, the smaller the possibility, humanly speaking, of fulfilling it as well as in the case of a man faced with a lesser post." [23]

LEADERSHIP AS A POWER POSITION

The official religious leader is called a superior, and from the point of view of social status this term refers to a superordinate position in the social structure as related to various subordinate positions. This is a superiority of position which in the terminology of social science is ascribed rather than achieved. Thus it does not necessarily imply superiority of personal talent or virtue. The fact that we talk about religious "subjects" rather than religious "inferiors" tends to bear out this contrast. The individual religious is subject to the authority of the superior; his status in the group is inferior to the status of the superior, but the personal traits or qualities of the individual may be not at all inferior.

The power attached to this superior position, sometimes called the authority of the superior, has also been called domestic power, economic power, social power, and finally by the Code itself *dominative* power. [24]

---

206. The notion that subjects' virtues should also be superiors' virtues is based on the fact that the Divine Master does not ask His followers to do anything that He Himself was not prepared to do.
    22. Rahner, *op. cit.*, p. 293.
    23. *Ibid.*, p. 292.

"This term takes its origin from that used to describe the relationship between a master and a servant brought on by a free agreement. Later it was used to describe the power in any imperfect society." The definition is as follows: "Dominative power is that private authority existing in at least every imperfect society arising from the very nature of the society, limited by its end and purpose, and embracing all who by a necessary relation or by an act of free will have become subject to it." [25]

Although the superior is said to take the place of God in the direction of religious subjects, the authority attached to this office is a limited one. "Unlike jurisdiction, dominative power is a private power dealing with a private group of persons. Therefore, it cannot be either executive, or judicial, or legislative; it is simply preceptive. In virtue of dominative power the superioress may command her subjects and direct them, urging the fulfillment of the constitutions and the rule." [26]

The limitations placed upon this power by the Canon Law, by the constitutions of the religious community, and indeed by the virtue of the incumbent himself, prevent this authority from becoming the naked and absolute power that Lord Acton feared and about which political groups are constantly concerned. As Bishop Roberts remarks, "the use of power is an issue vital in every generation. It has never been more urgent than today, in a world all but reduced to ruins by totalitarian abuse of authority." [27] A recommendation of the Holy Father, Pope Pius XII, seems to be pertinent here, when he says that in this day of machines and mechanical arts, "superiors are to be careful not to treat their subjects almost as merchandise or parts of a machine but they are always to respect the human person." [28]

Nevertheless it is an awesome thought to suggest that a human being stands in the place of God. One writer goes so far as to say that "in the ordinary course of events, appointment to the office of superior represents a fulfillment in time of an eternal decree." Indeed, St. Francis de Sales exclaimed on one occasion, "what a consolation for you that it is God Himself who has made you superioress!" [29] This may be the saint's way of indicating the fact that the position of authority does not derive from the personal traits or qualifications of the incumbent. It

29. Edward J. Carney, O.S.F.S., "St. Francis de Sales' Advice to Superiors," *Review for Religious,* vol. 14, (January, 1955), p. 15.

24. Canons 501, n. 1; 1312, n. 1.

25. Thomas Bowe, *op. cit.,* pp. 77, 79.

26. *Ibid.,* p. 80.

27. Archbishop Roberts, *Black Popes, Authority: Its Use and Abuse,* (New York: Sheed and Ward, 1954), p. 3.

28. Allocution to Teachers of the Order of Discalced Carmelites, *Acta Apostolicae Sedis,* vol. 43, (1951), p. 736.

may also be the reason why he recommended two basic virtues for superiors: "Humility and charity are the mainstays; all the other ropes are attached to them."

Under the notion that all authority comes ultimately from God, and in a cultural milieu where the concept of polyphasic authority was immediately suspect, it is easy to see how the position of superior came to be considered the position of God.[30] Religious communities, through their legislators and officeholders, found it simple and logical to transfer this notion from the ecclesiastical structure. The Roman Pontiff, as the official Vicar of Christ on earth, occupies the position of God. Under him, the bishops share in this position, and in a sense the priests too, who are called *alter Christus*. It is obvious, of course, that the superior of a religious group can never take the place of Christ in the same way that the Supreme Pontiff does.

The power position of the religious superior, however, is nothing without reference to the Pope and the Church. Both the mandate for apostolic works and the authority to carry out the mandate are derived from a juridical act of the competent authority of the Holy See. The religious Institute itself has a juridicial existence. "The Church herself is the founder, in a formal and strict sense of the term, of religious orders. The other founders and foundresses only furnish the matter. Competent ecclesiastical authority has made this matter its own, has given it a form and a canonical existence, and has determined its apostolic purpose." [31]

In speaking of the authority of superioresses, Gambari points out that it is not hierarchical or even indirectly episcopal in the sense of giving power over the faithful. It may, however, be termed ecclesiastical power. "Within her own Institute, the religious receives authority which, perhaps, could be considered ecclesiastical in this sense — that those religious who have been elevated to charges in the Institute possess real authority over the persons and things that belong to the Institute. Because of her mandate, the authority of the religious becomes somewhat similar to that of clerics, and we may say that her authority is ecclesiastical in this sense — that it comes to her from the Church and is exercised with a notable influence in the Church." [32]

---

30. "The superior in exercising her mandate is God's minister. She should appear in the eyes of her community as an image of God." Abbé Kothen, "The Superior, Servant of the Common Good," in Albert Plé, O.P. (ed.) *Religious Sisters,* (Westminster, Newman Press, 1954), p. 139.

31. Elio Gambari, S.M.M., "Recent Decrees of the Holy See Regarding the Apostolate," *Proceedings* of the 1957 Institute of Spirituality, Joseph Haley, ed., (Notre Dame: University of Notre Dame Press, 1958), p. 79.

32. Gambari, *op. cit.,* p. 83.

II

An Instrument of Social Control

Because the person in the superior's office wields authority he is often thought of as the one most responsible for "keeping order" in the group. Good order may be externally interpreted as the regular conformity of the membership to the accepted norms of behavior existing in the group.[1] In this sense the leader is the chief mechanism of social control. By the use of various sanctions, positive and negative, he gets the people to do what they are supposed to do.

Often enough, and unfortunately in the view of subjects, the central purpose of authority and power seems to be the enforcement of conformity. Penalties and negative sanctions tend to become synonymous with "good discipline," and to be associated with the main function of the superior. In its baldest and most negative form, this employment of social control ignores the desires of those who are controlled. The strict, authoritarian superior fails to recognize the relationship between knowledge and desire on the one hand, and voluntary, sustained behavior on the other. He focuses upon the motive of fear and not on the creative and positive motivation of the subject. This negative approach "requires constant supervision because it breeds an attitude which 'tries to get away with' whatever it can when the commander is not present."[2]

The negative drive to conformity also sometimes has other effects upon religious subjects, especially upon those who have an extraordinary amount of energy and zeal. As Everett Hughes remarks, "the ardor of a person with a peculiar mission may become an insufferable reproach to his colleagues and contain a trace of insubordination to his superiors. The neophyte who is too *exalté* can be borne, but a certain relaxation is

---

1. Although there must be order, and the power to command this order, says Rahner, religious obedience is not merely a "rational and inevitable regulation of traffic, by which every sensible person submits himself to the traffic policeman, and in which a coordinating agency takes care that everything moves without friction towards the common good." *Op. cit.*, p. 295.

2. See Ordway Tead, *Human Nature and Management,* (New York: McGraw-Hill, 1933), chap. 18, "The New Discipline," pp. 270-279.

demanded in course of time. In a well-established institution, ardor must be kept within the limits demanded by authority and decorum; it may not necessarily reach the state in which 'men, fearing to outdo their duty, leave it half done,' as Goldsmith said of the English clergy." [3]

It is because of this negative connotation that terms like authority and discipline have come into bad repute in everyday usage of the language. Discipline in the family, at school, and even on the job, is interpreted as the attempt to induce improvement in conduct by threats and penalties. It is even more frustrating when the alleged "improvement in conduct" is in reality an enforced conformity to lower goals in the hallowed name of prudence. Regardless of the direction in which the desired behavior moves, the inference in negative inducement is that the subject must either obey or suffer the consequences.

This type of social control may be followed by two unwanted results: frustration of the subject and failure of the superior. The subject is frustrated because he feels that he is simply being manipulated by a power outside himself and beyond the group. The subject minimizes the importance of self-control and self-direction because he feels that control of his behavior is really out of his own hands. Furthermore, frustration tends to create aggressive attitudes in the subject. He gets angry at the superior, and this neither promotes conformity nor increases the subject's docility.

The failure of the superior is seen in the fact that negative sanctions frequently do not really produce the kind of conformity desired by the superior. "If one is riding a horse it is wise to use the whip only if one holds the reins. Unless the superior controls every alternative form of behavior available to the subject, the resulting behavior may satisfy the subject but not the superior!" [4] A threat or an actual penalty may help to eliminate one kind of behavior, but the subject may substitute for it another equally undesirable behavior pattern. He may loaf, or sulk, or perhaps even go to the extreme of severing his connections with the community.

The ultimate expression of effective social control (unless it be the enforced conformity of the prison or concentration camp) must necessarily be the self-control of the subject. Otherwise, there is lost, or at least minimized, the tremendous source of self-discipline and of willing cooperation that exists within the individual and the group. This is some-

---

3. Everett Hughes, "Institutional Office and the Person," *American Journal of Sociology*, vol. 43, no. 3, (November, 1937), p. 408.
4. Douglas McGregor, "The Staff Function in Human Relations," *Journal of Social Issues*, vol. 4, no. 3 (Summer, 1948), pp. 6-23.

times called the "function of substitution" and in ascetical literature we read that the subordinate should strive to "make the superior's will his own." It seems particularly important in religious communities, where the good-will of the subject is waiting to be tapped, that the superior try to awaken this personal means of control that is internal to the group.[5]

The Abbé Kothen holds this as an attainable ideal when he says that the superior "should strive to reduce the weight of her authority by her efforts to render it unnecessary. Indeed the ideal way of exercising authority is not by multiplying orders and commands but on the contrary by minimizing them as far as possible. Thus a spirit is created in the community whereby the will of the superior is carried out spontaneously. It no longer is necessary to command."[6] This is, of course, never a one-sided proposition. The positive contribution of both the superior and the subject are assumed in this kind of ideal arrangement.

This is what good order and good discipline — those *desiderata* of religious life — really imply. Social conformity in any human group means an "orderly conduct of affairs by the members of an organization who adhere to its necessary regulations because they desire to cooperate harmoniously in forwarding the ends which the group has in view and willingly recognize that to do this their own wishes must be brought into reasonable unison with the requirements of the group in action."[7] Every reasonably intelligent being, and certainly every religious subject, has the normal desire to express himself in action, and this necessarily includes the willingness to put forth effort, to subordinate himself in a reasonable way, and to cooperate in group action.

The alternative to the strict authoritarian form of negative social control is the employment of positive sanctions for obtaining conformity.

---

5. "The subject in religious life has no right simply to take refuge behind obedience, as if he could thus be free from a responsibility which he himself must bear, the responsible direction of his own personal initiative. We often hear apologies of obedience which praises this supposed advantage. It does not exist." Rahner, *op. cit.*, p. 299.

6. Abbé Kothen, *op. cit.*, p. 142. A similar notion is expressed in an entirely different context. "The ideal personnel manager is always endeavoring to work himself out of a job. . . . Human inadequacy and executive and supervisory turnover leave such a man with no fear of being out of work but with his objective unchanged. Frequently, a personnel executive falls for the temptation to gather unto himself greater and greater authority and responsibility for human relations. The more he does so, the closer and closer he gets to the end of the limb." Lawrence A. Appley, "Essentials of a Management Personnel Policy," *Personnel,* vol. 23, no. 5, (May, 1947), pp. 430-436.

7. Ordway Tead, *op. cit.*

This is by no means simple or easy. It requires administrative talent of a high order, a kind of managerial tact and considerable ingenuity.[8] The superior who does not have this competence may slip readily into a sickening kind of paternalism. The direct provision of means of satisfaction for the subject, such as favors, permissions and exemptions, is typical of paternalistic management and does not achieve enduring results. The most effective forms of positive sanctions appear to be the provision of opportunities by means of which the subject *through his own efforts* achieves greater need satisfaction, conforms to the rules and gets his work done.[9]

Authority as a Social Relation

The obvious existence of social relations in this whole area of human activity hardly needs demonstration. Just as we cannot talk of superior status and higher power without inferring the lower status and subjection of the group member, so also must we realize that the superior as a person has a social relationship with the subject as a person. Indeed, obedience has been called a "vital relation" because the "one demanding obedience and the one performing obedience are fatefully bound to each other. To the weak or even wicked commander of obedience there corresponds the man who weakly or hypocritically accepts obedience." [10]

This relationship of the authoritative superior to the obedient subject is most often discussed from the point of view of the subject's duty in virtue of his weighty vow of obedience. An emphasis of this kind is to be expected since it is the superior, or his representative, who gives most of the conferences to the religious community. Nevertheless, "the responsibility of the one obeying is such a primary factor that it immediately and unhesitatingly challenges the absolute responsibility of the commander to the one obeying. And the gesture of trust of a subordinate laden with responsibility, who offers his person to a superior in obedience to God, calls for the personal response of the superior. It is absolutely

8. See the research conclusions of Douglas McGregor, *op. cit.*, who talks about augmentation and reduction of the individual's need satisfactions as the two main means used by superiors to change the behavior of subjects. See also Dale Yoder, *Personnel Principles and Policies,* (New York: Prentice-Hall, 1952), chap. 20, "Employee Motivation."

9. This is the management principle that avoids the deadening effects of paternalism. Similarly, "the office of government is not to confer happiness, but to give men opportunity to work out happiness for themselves." William Ellery Channing, *The Life and Character of Napoleon Bonaparte.*

10. Friedrich Heer, "The Rebirth of Catholic Obedience," *Cross Currents,* vol. 6, no. 2, (Spring, 1956), pp. 119-130.

impossible that a personal relationship of obedience should remain one-sided, that is, be answered by the superior merely officially and impersonally, according to administrative practices." [11]

We shall see later that the personal relationship of authority, as required in the familial organization of the religious community, presents a special problem when confronted by the need for a rational and functional exercise of authority in the professional, apostolic works of the community. The fact is, however, that in the religious community the relationship between superior and subject is clothed in the terminology of kinship. The Holy Father has said that the community "should take the place of the family as far as possible," and that superiors are "called to inspire the common life of the Sisters with the warmth of family affections." [12]

Archbishop Roberts points out that the *splendor caritatis* of the superior is meant to "combine a father's strength with a mother's tenderness and understanding of weakness." [13] In such a context it is perhaps natural that the superior wants his subject to have a feeling of personal loyalty and responsibility to him. Between the superioress and her subject the notion of the mother-daughter relationship implies that there will be an attitude of reverence, love, dependence and respect of the child to the mother.

One of the problems here is intimacy. The grown child in the ordinary family has many outside activities, relations and groups. In the religious community the whole life of the subject is bound up in the group and with the superior. It is hard to separate the home-life and the work-life, to distinguish between the superior as the mother of the community and as the principal of the school. The local community is usually a small operation. In the Fort Wayne diocese the convents attached to parochial schools average 6.95 members, and even in the cities where the schools are larger the religious community is still quite small. In the city of Fort Wayne itself the average number is 7.71, and in South Bend 8.13.

In a situation of this kind it is difficult to develop the impersonality of social relations that characterizes professional groups. It is difficult even to look upon one's spiritual mother as a kind of "grievance machin-

---

11. Hans Urs von Balthasar, *Bernanos,* quoted by Heer, *op. cit.,* p. 130.

12. Pope Pius XII, September 15, 1952, Address to the Congress of Mothers General, *Acta Apostolicae Sedis,* vol. 44, (1952), pp. 825-826. See the remarks of Abbé Baechler, "Open or Closed Community?", in Albert Plé, O.P., (ed.), *Communal Life,* (Westminster: Newman Press, 1957).

13. Archbishop Roberts: *Op. cit.,* p. 28.

ery" especially when the grievance may be against her as superior. The alternative in practice often seems to be a kind of paternalism. On the part of superiors this is an attitude that "mother knows best," and "you ought to trust me," and "you know that I have your interests at heart." It is expressed in pat formulae, in categorical answers, in rigid rules.

Paternalism in this sense is a form of immaturity on the part of the superior who expects and almost demands immaturity on the part of the subjects. People who have grown up in the American culture generally do not like to be "babied." If the training system of the religious community has made babies of the subjects; if they are kept immature and completely dependent, one may expect that the defect of paternalism will creep into the relationship of superior and subject.

It cannot be emphasized too strongly that the obedience characteristic of religious life is not even analogous to the obedience children owe to their parents. Children are immature, irresponsible, untrained, and in need of the educating influence of their older and wiser parents. Religious subjects are trained, responsible adults who are performing adult functions. When the Supreme Pontiff exhorted the mothers general to cultivate maternal sentiments and affections toward their subjects he was talking about a maternalism that "demands self-mastery," and therefore maturity.[14] Similarly, while paternal affection is desirable in the religious life of men, "the religious superior should not play the role of an Olympian papa." [15]

This question of the status of religious subjects is quite complex. Gambari implies that the religious is a child, remains a minor, is completely dependent, in both the juridical sense (that is, according to Canon Law) and in the ascetical sense (that is, depending completely on God, as represented by the religious superior.) He says also, however, that the religious sometimes has to act "as a really outstanding adult in other fields." [16] Perhaps it is in the field of apostolic functions, where the religious acts as a professional, that his adulthood must be recognized. The basic problems seem to be in all three areas — canonical, ascetical and professional — how the religious is supposed to behave like a child and at the same time the superior is not supposed to treat the religious like a child.

---

14. *Acta Apostolicae Sedis,* vol. 44, (1952), pp. 825-826.

15. Rahner, *op. cit.,* p. 293, also says that "superiors should cast a long and quiet glance at the world around them: Those who are truly powerful and influential, who receive a great deal of unquestioning obedience, place no value on ceremonial of this sort."

16. Gambari, *op. cit.,* p. 154.

From the point of view of the superior it seems necessary to distinguish between patriarchalism and paternalism, between formal and informal relations, between traditional and whimsical authority. Weber[17] and Toennies[18] talk about traditional and responsible patriarchalism as forms of authority existing in stable, communal organizations. Aside from the area of fixed customs in this system, however, there is also an area of paternalism, where arbitrary, *ad hoc* decisions are focused on personal relations with subjects. To the extent that the personal relation takes precedence over the functional relation, Weber would call it irrational authority, and we may well call it paternalistic authority.

The insufficiently mature superior is unhappy unless she gets from her subjects the responses that children theoretically owe to parents: the unquestioning recognition of authority and the demonstration of love and loyalty in exchange for parental protection and help. The problem breaks down to a kind of mutual immaturity. If it existed only in subjects, the problems it raises would be greatly simplified but "for every childish attitude in the private there is likely to be another in the captain, and the child in one has an unholy way of calling out the child in the other.[19]

Paternalism appears to be inherently vacillating and even ambivalent. It tends to range from excessive rigidity to excessive softness. It shows itself not so much as the result of the dictum that a person who cannot control himself cannot control others, but mainly as the result of emotional adolescence. Just as the adolescent's voice breaks, changes and cracks, so also is the voice of paternalistic authority constantly changing from softness to harshness and back again.

"The experience of directing others is strong drink: it warms the ego and puffs up one's sense of power. It is easy to slip into either of two alternatives: on the one hand using that power as an end in itself, becoming a little Mussolini in whatever station God has called us to; or, on the other, using authority as a means of buying gratitude, becoming what we accurately call paternalistic, interfering with the lives of less important people 'for their own good'." [20]

---

17. See H. H. Gerth and C. W. Mills, eds., *From Max Weber: Essays in Sociology,* (New York: Oxford University Press, 1946), pp. 294-299.

18. Ferdinand Toennies, *Community and Society,* (East Lansing, Michigan State University Press, 1952), pp. 41-42.

19. Smith Geddes, "The Adult: His Work," *Survey,* 1, vol. 60, (April 1, 1928), p. 34.

20. Smith Geddes, *op. cit.,* p. 34. Maturity implies of course, responsibility. "No man can climb to the summit of authority using the one leg of power. The other leg — responsibility — must go with him every inch of the way." Archbishop Roberts, *op. cit.,* p. 2. *Ecclesiastes,* 10:16, says, "Woe to thee, O land, when thy king is a child."

A SERVICE FUNCTION

The notion that the superior is the servant of his subjects is not a new one in the religious community. Christ Himself said, "I am here among you as your servant," (Luke 22:27) and the Holy Father himself has the proud title of the Servant of the Servants of God. In modern industrial organization this aspect of authority has been studied under the title of personnel administration, and it is clearly distinguished as a service function, rather than as a "doing" function. It is a service to those community members who get work out, that is, those who directly perform the external apostolic works of the congregation. [21]

It is unquestionably a function of the leader to help the follower wherever possible or necessary. If the leader's attempts are in any degree successful we can expect that the helper-helped relationship will develop into one in which the latter has some degree of dependence upon the former. "Although the Superior is a leader of the common good, she may not forget that the community she governs is composed of people, that is to say, of reasonable free beings, who are hence endowed with a certain amount of independence." [22]

The highest type of community relations between superior and subject, according to Toennies, is that which is based on unity of human wills. This most intense form of consensus is found in the relation between mother and child, husband and wife, brother and sister. "A superior power which is exercised *to the benefit of the subordinate* and which, because in accordance with his will, is accepted by him, I call dignity or authority. We distinguish three kinds: authority of age, authority of force, and authority of wisdom or spirit. These three are united in the authority of the father who is engaged in protecting, assisting and guiding the family." [23]

A very real problem arises in the religious community when the superior tries to make himself indispensable to the subject and, wittingly or unwittingly, fosters the subject's dependence. When this happens, the

---

21. Obviously in the small community no one can be "purely" an administrator, and in most instances the superior is also a "producer." As Father Philippe says, *op. cit.*, p. 18, "if she is Superior of a boarding school or a hospital, she must possess the technical competence needed for the administration of her establishment."

22. Marie-Therese Lemerle, O.S.U., "The Superior, Servant of the Common Good," in Albert Plé, O.P., (ed.) *Communal Life,* (Westminster: Newman Press, 1957), p. 297. She goes on to say what the superior ought to do in helping her subjects.

23. Ferdinand Toennies, *Community and Society,* tr. Charles P. Loomis, (Lansing: Michigan State University Press, (1957), p. 41.

superior's power in the relationship, and the subject's interpretation of that power, increase disproportionately. The subject gets to the point where he makes unreasonable demands on the superior for help. Then, no matter how unrealistic or unreasonable the subject's demands, any failure of the superior to provide the expected help is seen as a negative sanction or penalty by the subject." [24]

The goal of the superior's service is to strengthen the subject's competence rather than merely to placate him, and thus perhaps foster his dependence. The service of the top administrator in religious communities, the provincial or general, must be seen as something more than merely a "grease job" to keep the human parts of the organization operating smoothly. One provincial jokingly referred to himself as an "oil can" squirting lubricants on squeaking human relations. The question is whether the oil or grease used is the genuine remedy for deep-seated ailments. The misuse of curatives is reminiscent of the incident in *Alice in Wonderland* when the March Hare failed to repair the Mad Hatter's watch by smearing it with butter. The ineffectiveness of the remedy bewildered him and all he could repeat was, "and it was the *best* butter too, the *best* butter!"

FOCUS OF GROUP SOLIDARITY

It is a commonplace expectation that the religious community will develop to a high degree the solidarity, unity or cohesion which supposedly characterizes Christians as a group.[25] There are numerous and complex motives, incentives and factors involved in the development of this group solidarity, and not the least of these is leadership.[26] Just as the religious subject is frequently exhorted to develop a personal enthusiasm and loyalty to Christ, for Whom he is actually and ultimately working, so also may the superior be exhorted to "be like Christ," since he is taking the place of Christ.

Group solidarity is not an end in itself. It is not the passivity of the graveyard, nor is it "peace at any price," nor is it synonymous with cowering servility. Subjects are quick to recognize motives of expediency,

24. See Douglas McGregor, "The Staff Function in Human Relations," *Journal of Social Issues,* vol. 4, no. 3, (Summer, 1948), pp. 6-23.

25. Abbé Kothen, *op. cit.,* p. 135, suggests that religion itself is the strongest bond uniting people in society. "Consequently it is religious communities who should constitute the most perfect type of social solidarity."

26. One Jesuit indicates this as the soul of government: "The life of a woman superior is service. Her ideal is to bring about union of souls in charity." E. Bergh, S.J., "Government in Practice," in Albert Plé, O.P., *Religious Sisters,* (Westminster: Newman Press, 1954), p. 185.

intellectual dishonesty and cowardice in superiors. People generally prefer to be part of a group that is sparked and motivated by high ideals, and they also like to follow leaders who are imitable because they are committed to high ideals. At the same time, personal attachment to a leader, even though it helps to integrate the group, is sometimes a dubious quality in a follower. It is sometimes possible that the group is integrated because the members want to be like the central person, rather than because they accept the values for which he stands.[27]

There is no doubt that people are sometimes "united in their leader." This is a kind of *Fuehrerprinzip* that inspired the military followers of men like Napoleon and Lee. Some leaders are able to "rally people 'round," to develop group morale, to inspire and encourage followers. Without succumbing completely to the great-man theory as an exclusive principle of integration, one is still able to appreciate the enthusiasm and loyalty inspired in followers by the exceptional leader. He gets results. "There are countless testimonies and some degree of scientific data to support the conclusion that the greatest single factor of productivity of the individual is his mental attitude toward his boss." [28]

If we can trust the accounts of hagiography we can also discern large numbers of cases in which saints exercised a magnetic leadership among their followers. The small, faithful group at the beginning of many religious congregations consisted of people who were united not only through faith in a common cause and in common values but also through faith in a common leader. They were inspired by their dynamic leader to overcome all obstacles and to endure all hardships. We must remember that this concept of personal leadership was often based on the current notions of feudal dependence and personal fealty to a lord or chieftain. It is difficult for modern Americans to understand or to recapture this old-fashioned idea.

Nevertheless, it is true in modern times that a relationship exists between group solidarity and competent leadership. One may go so far as to say that successful leadership can be measured by the degree of enduring morale and social cohesion achieved by the group. One expert in this field insists that "high morale is the index of effective leadership.

---

27. On this point, see Fritz Redl, "Group Emotion and Leadership," *Psychiatry*, vol. 5, no. 4, (November, 1942), pp. 573-593, where he says that "they accept his authority because he sympathizes with their urges, or possibly illicit goals. Wanting to be like him establishes a common bond among the members, which furthers integration."

28. Thomas G. Spates, "Leadership and Human Relations at the Places where People Work," *Advanced Management*, vol. 13, no. 3, (September, 1948), pp. 98-102.

No success is possible without it. No failure is final unless it destroys morale, since morale is the emotional force that gives drive to group action. Morale is based on the belief of the leader in the follower, of the follower in the leader, of each in himself, and of both in the cause." [29]

As a rough rule-of-thumb to discover the degree of morale and solidarity among the members of the religious community, any superior might check the number of persons in his community who exhibit low morale. A person's morale is low when he is doubtful and suspicious, discouraged in the face of difficulty, thinking primarily of himself, doing as little work as possible in support of a cause to which he is not greatly devoted. The number of persons who follow this description may be explained by several other causes, but since one of the functions of leadership is to boost morale the failure of leadership may be the central cause.

In this whole delicate area of enthusiastic leadership and dedicated following a warning must be issued concerning imbalance. There is danger here of emphasizing the emotional reaction at the expense of the rational reaction of the follower. Identification with a successful leader, feeling pride in his success and sharing in his glory, tend to have emotional overtones. It may well be remembered, however, that human beings are not "pure intellects" and that they are impressed and influenced by what they like as well as by what they believe.

APOSTOLIC FUNCTION

Canonical commentaries appear to have little to say about the apostolic works of religious communities. Canon Law itself is intent upon regulating the internal organization of the religious group. "It is of the essence of the religious state that members of the community subject themselves to the direction of a higher authority. The consequence of this necessity has been the development of a canonical institute which provides stable offices in every religious community. Those elected or appointed to these offices are invested with the power necessary for governing the members of the community." [30]

In this context a religious superior is considered primarily as one who is "looking after the community," who keeps order in a smoothly running human organization. This is the basic reason why she has the office of authority, but it is also an overly-limited view of the facts of religious life in the American society. What appears necessary here is an inte-

29. Paul Pigors, *Leadership or Domination,* (New York: Houghton-Miffin, 1935), chapter 15, "Morale and Leadership," p. 291.

30. James Bowe, *op. cit.,* Foreword, p. vii.

grated focus on two matters that are commonly treated as separate or even conflicting goals: meeting the human problems of subjects and performing the works of the community.

It appears that both the internal and the external goals (if they can be so termed) of religious management are matters of common concern to both the subject and the superior. This is because they are all members of one working community, which was organized and maintained not only for the personal sanctification of members but also for the performance of the apostolic mission of the group. Thus the personal and the social aspects of community life are closely interwoven. Personal sanctification and apostolic work are mutually influential; each is a means to the other. The community exists for the purpose of getting the work of the Church done; it exists also as a means of meeting the spiritual needs of its members.[31]

This concept is so modern and important that it has been called "a new idea of religious life." The inexact terminology which called sanctification the "primary" end, and apostolic service to others the "secondary" end, has been abandoned. This terminology could give the impression that the apostolate is always something accessory to personal sanctification, whereas the fact is that the former specifies the latter. Gambari calls the apostolate the substantial element of personal sanctification which "is not simply added to or placed side by side to that which is traditional in the regular life of the search for personal sanctification, but has been inserted into the sanctification itself, imprinting a character on it, giving us our personal sanctification in the apostolate. The specific end has created the generic end." [32]

Experts in personnel administration have also made analogies along this line in other areas of group activity. The hospital does not exist only for its patients, but also for its personnel. The factory exists for the benefit of both its workers and its customers. The problems of people in the organization are inextricably interwoven with the problems of getting the organization's work done. The effective administration of personnel "releases energy, stimulates development, encourages teamwork,

---

31. Pope Pius XII points out that "an eager external activity and the cultivation of the interior life demand more than a bond of fellowship; as far at least as evaluation and willed effort are concerned, they demand that they should march along together step by step. . . . The Church insistently demands of you that your external works correspond to your interior life and that these two maintain a consistent balance." *Acta Apostolicae Sedis,* vol. 43, (1951), p. 32.

32. Gambari, *op. cit.,* p. 91. On this he cites Motu Proprio, *Primo Feliciter,* II, Comment. n. 161.

and helps with human problems." [33] Under these conditions subjects are more willing and better able to make their maximum contribution toward the "productive" aims of the community, that is, toward performing its external apostolic work. Such aims are then seen not as the demands of the superior, but as goals for all organizational members.

This has been a hard-won insight of social science research, and it is not yet fully accepted in the world of work. As Roethlisberger says, "to get maximum results, managers must think of more than results. They must understand the needs of the people on whom they depend for results." [34] Religious superiors who are intent upon maintaining both a happy and an efficient community may well profit from the research experience in economic organizations. "The administrator not only gets things done in the best known ways, but the people through whom he works to achieve results are made to feel that they are on the team and not just with it." [35]

---

33. Paul Pigors and Charles A. Myers, (ed.) *Readings in Personnel Administration,* (New York: McGraw-Hill, 1952), Preface, p. vi.

34. F. J. Roethlisberger, quoted by Pigors and Myers, *op. cit.,* p. 111.

35. Thomas G. Spates, *op. cit.,* p. 99.

III

Authority and Community

The term religious community has come to be applied to groups of people who, with the approval and under the guidance of the Church, live and work together in the service of the Church. Although the religious state has an important place in Canon Law, it was not brought into being by the law which constantly governs and protects it. "The religious life owes its birth to a spontaneous impulse of the Christian conscience. In the language of today we should say it has been produced by private initiative." [1] There has been evolution and change, and always the religious life "has been ahead of the law, forever giving birth to new forms." [2]

In attempting to discover how authority is or may be employed in religious communities performing the external apostolic work of the Church it seems advantageous to analyze the religious community from the point of view of social structure. This is a question of the organization of the religious group as a socio-cultural system, and it requires that we investigate various principles or modes of social organization.

The crux of the problem that we are facing in the structure of religious groups appears to be that the religious group is not organized according to any clear-cut or exclusive principle. The familial-communal mode of organization guides the *way of life* that the members follow in their daily domestic experience. The *system of authority* under which these people live seems to be derived mainly from the bureaucratic mode of organization. The *apostolic functions* they perform are mostly guided by the professional principle or organization. To put this in other words, the religious community is attempting to maintain and operate a group of professional people on the basis of a general bureaucratic system while

---

1. Jacques LeClercq, *The Religious Vocation*, (New York: Kenedy, 1955), p. 7.
2. The Apostolic Constitution, *Provida Mater Ecclesia*, February 2, 1947, remarks "In the course of the centuries, the Church, faithful to Christ her spouse, and in herself always the same, gradually developed, under the guidance of the Holy Spirit, with certain and uninterrupted steps, the discipline of the state of perfection, until our present Code of Canon Law was promulgated."

at the same time promoting the ideals of familial-communal way of life for these people.

A religious order, congregation or society, is in sociological terms a secondary association of people with numerous local communities, some of which may be called primary groups.[3] "The ideal type of the monastic community conforms to the type of a relatively small personalized group. The religious order, on the other hand, is a far more abstract and complex form of social organization."[4] This distinction is sociologically significant from the point of view of structure. Another important distinction is that between the "kinds of houses," or local communities: those that are basically training places — like novitiates and houses of study — and those that are the functioning missions — the places where the apostolic work of the order gets done. Most of our comments will be concerned with the latter.

FAMILY AND COMMUNITY

People who are formally organized in the religious life are most frequently called a religious community or a religious family, but it must be said that from a strictly technical and sociological point of view this group is neither a family nor a community. The best we can say is that it is analogous to a familial-communal form of organization, being in some ways similar, and in other ways dissimilar, to both the family and the community.

Any introductory textbook in sociology will provide a working definition of the family, and will also usually distinguish between the conjugal, or nuclear, family and the consanguine, or extended kinship system. In either case, the family combines two basic functions. "It controls sexual behavior for purposes of reproduction, and it provides for the organic social development of offspring. As a social institution, it is characterized by common residence, economic cooperation, and reproduction. These distinctive functions — sexual, reproductive, educational, and economic — invest the family with a many-sided utility rendering its universality inevitable."[5]

The analogy between the religious group and the family is brought out by Abbé Baechler. "First and foremost the family works to procure the good of its members: it brings them into the world, feeds them,

---

3. See Joseph H. Fichter, *Sociology,* (Chicago: University of Chicago Press, 1957), pp. 117-118.
4. E. K. Francis, "Toward a Typology of Religious Orders," *The American Journal of Sociology,* vol. 55, no. 5, (March, 1950), pp. 437-449.
5. John Thomas, *The American Catholic Family,* (Englewood Cliffs, Prentice-Hall, 1956), p. 3.

shelters them, educates them, makes it possible for them to fulfill their earthly and their eternal destiny. Next, it procures the good of society: the interior activity of the family runs parallel with an exterior activity, which may be professional, intellectual, civic, etc., but is indispensable to the human community. Thus, we observe simultaneously in the family a private life which must be guarded with care and a social influence which must be cultivated to yield more and more fruit." [6]

Sociological literature is replete with definitions and descriptions of the human community, although the term is widely and popularly used also in non-technical meanings. Interest in this concept is being aroused now among those who feel that the "breakdown of community" is the great crisis of modern Western society. One enthusiastic author goes so far as to say that "the first purpose of monasteries today is to bear witness before the Church and the world of the necessity of community life." [7]

A community may be defined as a group of neighbors who have frequent primary relations, function cooperatively in their main activities, have a sense of group identity, and share in common values.[8] Redfield points out that there is a quality of homogeneity as well as of self-sufficiency about the typical small community.[9] In his classic work on *Gemeinschaft*, Toennies says that the "truly human and supreme form" of community is had when a consensus of mind and will is added to the unity of kinship and locality.[10]

There are certain characteristics which the local religious community shares with the family and the community, as described above. (a) It is

---

6. Abbé Baechler, "Open or Closed Community?" in Albert Plé, O.P., (ed.) *Communal Life*, (Westminster: Newman, 1957), p. 199.

7. R. Schutz, *Introduction a la Vie Communautaire*, p. 29, quoted by Abbé Kothen, *op. cit.*, p. 136, who appears to be deeply upset about the profound evil of social disintegration, the proletarization of the masses, and thinks that we have touched the bottom of the abyss of atomization.

8. See Baker Brownell, *The Human Community*, (New York: Harper, 1950), Part 8, "The Nature of Community"; John A. Kinneman, *The Community in American Society*, (New York: Appleton-Century-Crofts, 1947), p. 4, who says that the three significant elements are territory, group of people and common culture; Carle C. Zimmermann, *The Changing Community*, (New York: Harper, 1938), p. 15; also Jesse F. Steiner, *Community Organization*, (New York: Appleton-Century, 1930), p. 23, who stresses the unity of common economic pursuits rather than the bond of kinship.

9. Robert Redfield, *The Little Community*, (Chicago: University of Chicago Press, 1955), p. 4.

10. Ferdinand Toennies, *op. cit.*, p. 47. Consensus, or understanding, is the reciprocal binding sentiment of the community, keeping the members together as a totality. "Understanding is based upon intimate knowledge of each other insofar as this is conditioned and advanced by direct interest of one being in the life of another, and readiness to take part in his joy and sorrow."

relatively small in numbers of members. For example, the normal Sisters' convent attached to a parochial school, having seven or eight members, is fairly large as a family and very small as a community. (b) Because of its small size the religious group tends to have frequent, *face-to-face relations* and primary contacts among its members. (c) The convent tends to be fixed in one place over a fairly long period of time, and is thus *identified*, even though some of its personnel may come and go from year to year. (d) The members typically have a *sense of solidarity* and of loyalty to the group. (e) They also have a *consensus of values* in that they share similar basic ideals. (f) Finally, the religious group is one in which the way of life, the patterns of behavior, *change slowly*.

DISSIMILARITIES

The three kinds of social organization that we have been discussing — the family, the lay community, the religious community — typically share the above characteristics. These are some, but by no means all, of the elements found in the communal, as compared to the associational type of society.[11] Since we are making a comparison among three types of groups, we may note also that there are certain aspects of resemblance between the family and the lay community which the religious community does not share, and also similarities between the family and the religious community which are not present in the lay community.

Following is a series of characteristics which mark the religious community, but which are not present in either the family or the lay community. (a) The religious community, whether on the local or the provincial level, is made up of *only one sex*. (b) In *age composition* also the religious community differs because it has an age minimum as an entrance requirement and contains no children. (c) The membership and participation in the local particular religious convent is *temporary* in the sense that some part of the personnel may be changed annually. The religious members come and go, while the members of family and lay community remain fairly stable. (d) The social relations of the religious members are expected to be more or less *impersonal* in the sense that cliques, primary sub-groups and particular friendships are discouraged. (e) The behavior patterns of religious members are governed largely by formal rules, detailed and written, while those of the family and community are governed more by the mores and folkways of the group. (f) Because of these rules and regulations, and the training provided in their pursuit, the daily religious life tends to be marked by *social for-*

---

11. See Joseph H. Fichter, *Sociology*, (Chicago: University of Chicago Press, 1954), pp. 139-142.

mality, in contrast to the informality one finds in the family and the lay community. (g) Membership in the religious group is *voluntary* in the broad sense that the individual person elects to join the group and to remain in it. On the other hand one is born into a family and a community, and at least during his younger years has little freedom to depart from it. (h) The functions performed in the religious group are, ideally at least, *common tasks,* while those in the community and the family are almost necessarily diverse.

When we further analyze this triple contrast of family, lay community and religious community, we find still another combination of elements present in the family and the religious group, but not in the lay community. (a) The lay community, as studied by social scientists, is typically *self-sufficient,* while the family and the religious groups are incomplete and dependent groups. (b) Even the smallest lay community is composed of a number of *sub-groups,* while the family and the religious community are not so sub-divided. (c) The lay community operates generally under *diffused power,* while the family and the religious group are each under a centralized authority. (d) Membership in the family and the religious group is *individual and personal,* while that in the lay community is a group-membership in the sense that the lay community is made up of families rather than of individuals.

There remain several characteristics of the social group that are different in all three of the groups under discussion. (a) There is typically *little stratification* in any of these three forms of association, but what does exist in the religious group is mainly that of seniority, while by the achievement of all of the various criteria of status in the lay community by age, sex, and function. (b) The religious group has at best a simulated *kinship* arrangement, while the family is a genuine single kinship group, and the community is typically made up of a plurality of families. (c) Upward *social mobility* is also little in evidence in all three groups. Status, however, tends to be ascribed in the religious community; it is achieved by the assumption of new roles in the family, and by the achievement of all of the various criteria of status in the lay community. (d) Finally, the *locus of authority* in the religious group is found in the official position of the superior, while in the family it is traditionally in the person of the father, and in the community it is typically in all of the adults or elders.

The purpose in isolating these social characteristics and in making a comparison among the three types of social groups has not been merely a demonstration of taxonomic virtuosity. When we put all of these elements together we find that the local convent, or religious community, is like nothing else on earth. In its totality, it is not and cannot be either a family or a lay community. It is unique in its structure because it is unique in its purposes, and because it has been artificially contrived by human beings, who after all, are endowed with the ability to fashion and maintain a great variety of human groups.

MAINTENANCE OF THE GROUP

The exercise of authority is concerned with the structural characteristics of the religious community from two points of view: first, the maintenance of the group as a going concern, and secondly, the performance of the work for which the group was established.[12] Involved in both of these questions is, of course, the twofold human goal of the group: the satisfaction of the social needs of the group members themselves, and the satisfaction of the social needs of the "clients" or beneficiaries, to whom the group is giving service.

At this point in our analysis we are concerned only with the manner in which authority is related to the maintenance of this peculiar kind of social group, the local religious community. On the surface, it appears that this kind of group ought to be easy to manage, and that the exercise of authority ought to be smoother and more efficient than in either the family or the lay community. If we rearrange all of the social characteristics and discuss them from this point of view we may consider them in four categories: (1) the composition of the group, (2) the type of authority; (3) solidarity of the members, and (4) social relations.

(1) The fact that the local convent is relatively small contributes to simplicity and ease of management. All other things being equal, a small group is easier to administer than a large group. Similarly, the fact that the group is only of one sex, and that the members are to this extent culturally alike, makes for fewer difficulties in management. Since there are no children in the group, the disturbing element of partially socialized persons who are still learning the virtues of obedience and conformity, is removed.[13]

(2) The kind of authority and the way in which it operates also constitute an advantage in maintaining the group. The members understand quite clearly that there is only one authority in the house and

---

12. These are the minimum essentials for any group: that it maintain itself in existence and that it produce the results for which it exists. Obviously, both of these are a matter of degree. See Elton Mayo, *The Social Problems of an Industrial Civilization,* (Cambridge: Harvard University Press, 1945), p. 9, who uses slightly different terms.

13. Obviously, there may be significant variations in the moral and psychological qualities of community members. We can merely assume at this point that the selectivity of the novitiate and the training of members have led to the previous elimination from the organization of clearly unfit and deviant personalities.

they are conditioned to the notion (even though they may not always act upon it) that the personal faults and idiosyncrasies of the superior do not detract from her position of power.

One of the important components in the exercise of authority here is that a body of clear-cut and formal rules exists, which are known to all of the members and to which they have given assent. They have accepted these regulations, and they know the limitations of the superior's authority. In most aspects of their behavior there is no ambiguity as to what constitutes following or breaking the rules. The influence of both the superior and the rules ought to be advantageous from the further fact that both represent a repetitive pattern of behavior. This is another way of saying that sudden shifts and changes are unlikely. The relatively unchanging aspect of authority and rules tends to lend stability and permanence to the group.

(3) A much more important factor in the maintenance of the group appears to lie in the social solidarity that is expected of the members. These people have not been impounded into the community. They are voluntary members who are giving their whole lives freely to the group. They are united to the group at least in a simulated kind of kinship where the nomenclature of sister and mother is constantly used and ought to help develop a sense of familial unity. Furthermore, the striving for upward mobility, which is a characteristic of the American social structure and which implies social competition and personal ambition, is supposedly absent in this group. Thus, one of the main obstacles to peaceful cooperation is removed from the religious community.

Since social stratification is present in every kind of group we cannot expect the religious community to be an exception. The difference here, however, is that the only official higher status is that of the superior, and that social status is otherwise gained among the members by seniority and perhaps by personal charm and friendliness. The two principal factors of solidarity appear to be the acceptance of shared values and the performance of common tasks. Loyalty to the group is maintained by the fact that the members not only share the same religious values but also the "community spirit" peculiar to each religious order. Even more important is the solidaristic consequence of common tasks.[14] When

---

14. The theological virtues, especially charity, must be assumed throughout this discussion as contained among the shared values. Attention may be called, however, to individuals who miss the social implications of their religious role. "Intent upon their own personal perfection rather than on charity, they live a very individualistic and insulated life." Bernard I. Mullahy, C.S.C., "Community Life," *Review for Religious,* vol. 14, (May, 1955), p. 147.

people do together the things they think are worth doing they are almost inevitably drawn into closer unity as a group.

(4) The familiarity of the members with one another is tempered by the kind of social relations they have, and this too makes authority easier. Ordinarily in the primary group, frequent face-to-face relations develop in an atmosphere of informality. In the religious community a deliberate attempt is made to keep these relations on a relatively formal and impersonal basis. The purpose of this formality and impersonality appears to be the prevention of frictions that might be engendered by the close confines of the small community. Loyalty to the group may be weakened if close devotion develops between two or more members. Friendship pairs and triads may arise which "split" the group.

In a sense it may be a paradox that the member is treated as an individual who has an intelligent understanding of her relation to the other members of the group and at the same time is expected to have a close union with the group through the virtue of charity. Yet it is always true that each member is ultimately responsible to a higher superior for her own behavior. She is close to the others and must still stand apart and not depend too much upon them. If for some reason, whether due to herself or to some outside factor, she does not "fit in" to the group, there is always the possibility that she may transfer to another community in the following year. Thus, the transient character of the social relations within the group is an element that helps positively to maintain the group as a whole.

We must recall here that we have been considering the religious community only from the point of view of its internal maintenance as a group. We have not yet analyzed it from the point of view of its apostolic function. What has been said above indicates that the religious group ought to be easy to administer, that it ought to be a close-knit solidaristic group. It is small and stable. The members have a loyalty and solidarity based on common tasks, objectives and values. People have willingly left other careers and pursuits and other kinds of social groups in order to dedicate themselves to God in this religious community.

IV

Performance of Apostolic Function

We must now face the fact that there are also certain disfunctional elements in the modern religious community when we analyze it in the light of its corporate service to the Church. We are, of course, discussing only the local religious group that has a public function to perform in the Church's apostolate, and not one that is completely set off from the world. This group also, as we have seen, ordinarily forms a segment of a larger total organization, the secondary association or congregation.

Under these conditions the small convent that looks so peaceful and cohesive when viewed only from its internal structure, begins to take on a remarkably different appearance. The community is pulled now in two directions. Because of its segmental position in a large complex structure it is pulled toward the bureaucratic form of organization. Because of its function in the public apostolate of the Church it is pulled toward the professional mode of organization. The bureaucratic and professional forms of organization not only differ from one another; they differ also from the religious type of local community we have described above.

At the risk of oversimplification (which may be amplified in the later discussion) we may say that the central difference between the bureaucratic and the professional modes of organization is that the former emphasizes a procedural orientation and the latter a functional orientation. Both modes put a premium on efficiency in the sense that they are arranged in order to get the work out in the way best possible with the means at hand.[1] The "set way" of doing things that has been tested over long periods of time is characteristic of the bureaucracy. The

---

1. The Sacred Congregation of Religious hints at the combination of both aspects in saying that the most strict obligation of the teaching Sisters is "to labor for the good of their own institute and to contribute efficaciously to the apostolate of the Church." To this end it urges "the mothers general to make every effort to accomplish not only the formation of the young Sisters in the spirit of their institute but also their pedagogical and professional preparation." *Commentarium pro Religionis, Acta Apostolicae Sedis,* vol. 30. (1951), pp. 262-263.

"better way" of doing things that results from the skillful and proficient person is the characteristic of the professional mode of organization.

The difference has been succinctly stated as follows: "The bureaucratic mode emphasizes the system of organization and the subordination of the individual to it, whereas the professional mode emphasizes the role of the individual and subordinates the system of organization to individual activities and colleague relations. The bureaucratic principle centers on the relations of persons to one another by means of the system, whereas the professional principle centers on the relation of the individual to his work." [2]

Given the traditional and complex organization in which many religious orders operate, and given the fact that these orders are seriously attempting to do a professional job in their apostolic endeavors, one can readily perceive the seeds of their conflict. It may be said quite bluntly that sometimes the traditional procedures get in the way of the professional achievement, and sometimes the work gets in the way of the procedures. "Above all, what an evil it would be for religious and for the works undertaken by them if, setting their face deliberately against the most imperative demands of the world in which they live, they claimed to attach their search for perfection and subordinate their apostolic labors to ways and ideas of life now manifestly obsolete." [3]

Ideally, of course, there is meant to be a close connection between the regulations and the apostolic works, and there probably was in the mind of the Founder at the time he established the religious group. These observances "are not drawn up without reference to the apostolic works which form the end of the institute. It is indeed here that we find one of the principal justifications of the variety, if not of the endless multiplication, of religious rules. Not only must observances be compatible with the carrying out of the various works of charity undertaken, but they aim at placing the religious in that form of holiness most in harmony with the performance of the said works." [4]

Perhaps the best-known of the forceful expressions concerning "getting the work out" is that of Ignatius Loyola. The Jesuits have a reputation, deserved or not, for rationality, practicality and efficiency. Having

---

2. Roy G. Francis and Robert C. Stone, *Service and Procedure in Bureaucracy*, (Minneapolis: University of Minnesota Press, 1956), p. 157. For a historical and sociological analysis, see A. M. Carr-Saunders and P. A. Wilson, "Professions," *Encyclopaedia of Social Sciences*, vol. 12, pp. 476-480.
3. Dom Basset, "Observances, Prayer and Liturgical Life," in Albert Plé, O.P. (ed.) *Religious Sisters*, (Westminster: Newman Press, 1954), pp. 89-90.
4. *Ibid.*, p. 84.

a pure intention and following the regulations are of the utmost importance for Loyola and his followers, but these are interpreted as means for achieving success in the work of the Church. "To achieve the greatest possible success, a purposive rational method is adopted which is ever ready to re-examine traditional standards. Thus the original liturgical functions of the community of religious are now completely abolished as a hindrance to effective work. This rationality is also shown in the realistic consideration given to concrete conditions and to the prospects of any given procedure." [5]

BUREAUCRACY AND RELIGIOUS LIFE

To the unsophisticated person whose knowledge of social science may be quite superficial, bureaucracy has come to have a distasteful connotation. This is unfortunate because bureaucracies are not only omnipresent wherever large-scale social structures are in operation, they are also necessary if the operation is to be efficient. The factory is a bureaucratic organization, so is the government, the large city school system, the Church itself and its largest religious orders. "The type of organization designed to accomplish large-scale administrative tasks by systematically coordinating the work of many individuals is called a bureaucracy." [6]

In reference to the religious congregation the list of bureaucratic characteristics given here[7] must be analyzed from the point of view of the local religious community and its functioning members. In other words, the effect of the total bureaucratic organization reaches down to the smallest local group even though the structure of the latter is not typically bureaucratic in itself. The local community is "under" and "part of" the total bureaucratic structure because the ultimate "hands"

---

5. Gustave Gundlach, *Zur Soziologie der katholischen Ideenwelt und des Jesuitenordens,* (Freiburg: Herder, 1927), pp. 98-100, points out that the Jesuit idea of work comes close to that of Capitalism as understood by Max Weber and his school. Quoted by E. K. Francis, *op. cit.,* p. 447.

6. Peter M. Blau, *Bureaucracy in Modern Society,* (New York: Random House, 1956), p. 14.

7. The classic work on bureaucracy, from which all modern commentators take their start, is that of Max Weber. See, for example, Max Weber, *The Theory of Social and Economic Organization,* (New York: Oxford University Press, 1947), pp. 329-341. Translated by A. M. Henderson and Talcott Parsons. For a modern analysis of this concept see Philip Selznick, "An Approach to a Theory of Bureaucracy," *American Sociological Review,* vol. 8, no. 1, (February, 1943), pp. 47-54; Robert K. Merton, *et. al., Reader in Bureaucracy,* (Glencoe: Free Press, 1952); Reinhard Bendix, "Bureaucracy: The Problem and Its Setting," *American Sociological Review,* vol. 12, no. 5, (October, 1947), pp. 493-507.

and the work-producing units of the total organization are precisely these local convents.

a) The typical bureaucracy has an orderly, hierarchical *centraliza- .tion of power* in the sense that the grades of authority can be traced upwards and downwards. This is true even in a democratic form of organization, and it makes no difference whether the offices are elective, appointive or usurped. There is little direct contact between the top man and the rank-and-file.

b) The bureaucracy *emphasizes rules,* procedures, patterns, that have become formalized from frequent and traditional repetition. Even though change is allowed and necessary, the change is imposed from above and the new "set way" becomes as sacred as the old. This is an important aspect of the system because precise procedure tends to become almost an end in itself.[8]

c) The secret of efficiency in the bureaucracy is the specialization and *simplification of individual tasks* because each task is seen only as one segment of the whole. This is one of the reasons for proliferation of the bureaucracy: major, complicated tasks are broken down into simple, repetitive units of work and distributed to people who can do each simple section of the work. Theoretically people are replaceable (at least in the lower echelons) because the thinking has been done for them.

d) This means that *relatively little initiative* is allowed to the individual persons in the bureaucratic form of organization. All tasks and activities have been prearranged and interlocked, and the whole system would get out of gear if the individuals tried to do things "their own way." Thus the worker is not expected to think for himself.

e) In the bureaucracy there tends to be a *corporate responsibility* in the sense that it is the system itself and as a whole that gets the work done.[9] This is why the "system" carries the weight of blame and is so often actually blamed by individuals when things go wrong. It is particularly difficult for the people at the lower strata of the organization to locate the blame in any person or office higher up.

f) *Impersonality* is also a frequently noted characteristic of the bureaucracy. This is logically to be expected more in vertical social rela-

---

8. This impersonal aspect was criticized by Pope Pius XII, when he told the Roman Pastors that "you should be on your guard against an excessive bureaucracy in the care of souls." *Acta Apostolicae Sedis,* vol. 43, (1951), p. 116.

9. "It is this pattern that is actually productive, not the individual. Modern industry requires a group organization far exceeding in forethought, precision and cohesion anything we have ever witnessed before." Peter Drucker, *The New Society,* (New York: Harper, 1949), p. 22.

tions than in horizontal relations. It is a reflection of the fact that the task performed is more important than the person performing it, and also of the fact that impersonality prevents sentimentality, favoritism and nepotism in the selection and retention of personnel.

g) A further consequence of the bureaucratic system is that the status of the person is mainly a *status of ascription*. Since the relative position of any person is fixed on an organizational basis, the prestige any person enjoys is mainly the prestige of the office he holds and only secondarily the result of personal qualities and achievement.

h) Finally, in a bureaucracy emphasis is placed on the fact that the individual *serves the organization*. In spite of the obvious fact that the organization as a whole must successfully "serve the public" — no matter what its general function may be — the individual member must be dedicated and loyal to the organization itself.[10] He works for it, while it works for the public.

It is probable that the ordinary rank-and-file member of a religious community sometimes thinks of himself as being caught up in this kind of a bureaucratic system. In varying degrees he has noticed how rules and regulations seem to be emphasized for their own sake, how he is sometimes treated like a child without responsibility or initiative or other personal competences, how the major superior who could do something about it seems so remote and impersonal, how the good of the organization and its service seem to override local and personal needs. The religious subject may be only vaguely conscious of the institutionalized source of such troubled thoughts. He may even have feelings of guilt for giving in to the temptation of entertaining such thoughts.

PROFESSIONAL MODE OF ORGANIZATION

The problems growing from the bureaucratic system of organization are certain to increase as more and more religious receive thorough training and develop proficiency in their specialized type of apostolic work. Some modification of the bureaucracy is almost inevitable if the counsel of the Holy Father is to be followed and if the public works of the religious community are to be equal to, or even better than, similar works performed by parallel lay organizations.

"The professional mode of organization seems to stem from the relation of the individual to a specialized type of work. The professional

---

10. A penetrating and somewhat negative analysis of this concept is found in William H. Whyte, *The Organization Man,* (New York: Simon and Schuster, 1956).

principle implies a group of individuals involved in carrying out a special activity in which high skills are wielded, and where the major goal is service either to clients or a public. As a result of long training and indoctrination with a code, members of the group are considered individually responsible. Consequently great stress is placed upon colleague relations in which the individuals are equal. Respect for the skills of others is an integral part of the colleague relation." [11]

a) In the professional type of organization there tends to be a diffused *leadership of expertness*. The functionary becomes an "authority" in his field, and for this reason has influence over others. Even though there are recognized ranks according to skill and knowledge, the superior professional tends to be fairly close to his subordinates.

b) The professional system of organization necessarily *allows variability* in the sense that the functionary must be guided by the rules of the function rather than by the rules of the organization. The professional form allows much more leeway because the professional sometimes has to make decisions on the spot and to change his way of doing things when necessary.

c) The task of the professional is of such nature that it cannot be simplified and routinized. He tends to see *each task as a whole,* all of which he has to perform, and which he cannot easily break down into numerous simple and repetitive units of action.

d) The professional form of organization *encourages initiative* in the functionary. This comes from the fact that it is the expert in the field, and not the manager of the organization, who knows best when and how to make innovations. Progress in the service or the action performed can be expected only when the functionary is allowed to experiment.

e) Obviously, this kind of system places *personal responsibility* upon the professional who can be readily identified as the one who performs the central tasks. From this point of view he must answer first to himself for what he does, and then only afterwards to his clients, his associates and his superior.

f) The professional type of organization calls for good *personal relations* among the members of the organization, particularly among colleagues who are performing the same general kind of action or service, as well as between the professional superior and subordinate. The fact is, of course, that the social distance between any two positions in the system is not very great.

---

11. Francis and Stone, *op. cit.,* p. 156.

g) The prestige of the professional worker is primarily an *achieved status,* rather than an ascribed status. This means that the individual is appreciated for what he knows and does rather than for what official position he holds in relation to others. In the last analysis it is the productive role that counts in this type of organization.

h) From a sociological point of view the focus of attention must be placed on the fact that the worker *serves the client.*[12] Keeping the organization in operation is a means of helping the professional to perform the function for which the organization was formed. This is probably the crucial difference between the bureaucratic and the professional mode of organization and it is probably the "area of anguish" for the conscientious person who feels himself pulled between duty to the organization and duty to the public he serves.

A consideration of these characteristics of the professional mode of organization seems pertinent to the religious orders in America at a time when they are being urged to improve the quality and extent of their apostolic functions. The central danger seems to be that professionalism will foster a spirit of independence among the functionaries of religious groups. A peculiar problem is added here for the persons who become eminent in their particular fields. Their achievement is genuinely evaluated only by members of their profession — not by superiors in their religious community — and they thus attain prestige in an "outside" group that knows nothing of the interior operation of the religious order.[13]

This twofold relationship of the religious subject to his professional function and to the expectations of his professional colleagues constitutes a difficulty that has hardly been discussed, much less solved.[14] It involves an apparent conflict between the role of religious subject and the role of professional expert. It places the religious superior in a dilemma of a

---

12. There appears to be some theoretical uncertainty concerning the way in which this characteristic occurs. It appears that service to the client may be direct or indirect. Everett Hughes, "Psychology, Science and/or Profession?" *American Psychologist,* völ. 7, no. 8, (August, 1952), pp. 441-443, indicates that a profession necessarily implies service to a client.

13. Any systematic kind of rating by non-professionals is sharply disapproved, and the "determination of merit is entirely in the hands of fellow-professionals, at least in principle." See Theodore Caplow, *The Sociology of Work,* (Minneapolis: University of Minnesota Press, 1954), p. 110.

14. The characteristics of the professional role, as discussed here, are only one aspect of the study of professions. See for example, Caplow, *op. cit.,* chap. 5, "Occupational Institutions," where he discusses professions from various points of view: manner of recruiting, evaluation of seniority, evaluation of merit, control of occupational behavior, control of extraoccupational behavior, formation of occupational attitudes, internal ethos, external ethos, rate of growth or decline.

person who does not want what he has to have. It raises the question whether the traditional relationship between religious superior and subject —and indeed whether the whole structure of the religious order — can be maintained in the same way as of old.

TRIPLE MODE OF ORGANIZATION

The observations we have made about the bureaucratic and professional principles of organization have been simplified and handled separately for purposes of clarity and analysis. In the concrete, everyday operation of on-going organizations, one never finds either principle in its "pure state" or in the "ideal type" described above. Although there appears to be contrast, and even conflict, between the two principles, "we should remind ourselves that any mode of organization may contain both of these opposing principles in varying degrees and varying combinations. Furthermore, various segments or levels of a given institutional group may place different emphases upon these principles." [15]

Research data are now available to demonstrate that various combinations of bureaucratic and professional principles are found in almost any large organization and that they tend to intermesh in a workable fashion. "Academic persons recognize that in American universities certain segments of the system are run with emphasis upon bureaucratic modes of organization, but with reference to the activities of the faculty professional modes receive major emphasis.[16] In factory organization the employment of engineers, accountants, and other staff groups interjects into the system persons whose training and experience orient them toward the professional mode.[17] The modern large hospital is perhaps a classic example of the combination of bureaucratic and professional principles." [18]

It must be pointed out, however, that in none of these examples is there the intrusion of a third principle of organization, that of the local religious community. This is where the people who belong to an active religious community are involved in a unique social structure. The main

---

15. Francis and Stone, *op. cit.,* p. 157. See especially Talcott Parsons, *Essays in Sociological Theory,* (rev. ed.) (Glencoe: Free Press, 1954), chap. 2, "The Professions and Social Structure."

16. See Logan Wilson, *The Academic Man,* (New York: Oxford University Press, 1942), chap. 5.

17. Burleigh H. Gardner and David G. Moore, *Human Relations in Industry,* (Homewood: Irwin, 1952), chap. 6.

18. See Francis and Stone, *op. cit.,* pp. 157-158, and especially the whole of chap. 11, "Reassessment of the Concept of Bureaucracy": also *Nursing Service in a Premature Infant Center,* (New Orleans: Tulane University, 1953).

problem of structure appears to be that they are attempting to enact in the same group three social roles that people ordinarily enact in three separate groups. Roughly speaking, we may say that they are playing the family role, the religious role, and the occupational role, more or less simultaneously with the same people in the same group.

It would be gratuitous to suggest that only one of the alternative roles can be emphasized. In the context of the religious life and the apostolic function one cannot say that a choice must be made among the possibilities: a good community member, a holy religious, a professional functionary. The ideal to be striven for appears to be a combination of all three. It remains the task of religious leadership in the various religious congregations to investigate the ways in which the present social structure of religious congregations interferes with this ideal. At the present time it appears that the structure and organization require a reformation, and this seems to be what the Holy Father is constantly hinting at when he asks for adaptation.[19]

---

19. See the two excellent studies by Victor de la Vierge, O.C.D., "The Problem of Adaptation at the Present Day," and "Applications of the Principle of Adaptation," in Albert Plé, O.P. (ed.), *Religious Sisters*, (Westminster, Newman, 1954).

V

Authority and Apostolic Functions

The difference between the active and the contemplative life, and the combination of the two, have been so thoroughly discussed in ascetical literature that they need hardly be handled in detail. The nature of the apostolic life, however, does not appear to be so clearly understood. No less a person than the Holy Father has let it be known that the term "apostolic" is not to be limited only to the external works of the Church. "Let all cloistered religious know then that their vocation is fully and completely apostolic, in no way confined by boundaries of places, of things or of time, but extending everywhere and at all times, to everything with which it is related, in whatever way this may be, for the honor of their Spouse or the salvation of souls." [1]

It is possible nevertheless to analyze separately the active external apostolate of the religious congregation without denying the existence of the contemplative monastic apostolate. If we look at the modern religious community, not only as a means of individual self-perfection, but also as a service agency of the Catholic Church, we find that its most general goal is the salvation of society. This means that all the particularized missions and external works, like teaching and nursing and social work, are pointed at the elevation and improvement of people in society. The apostolic relationship between the religious community and the "outside" society in which it exists is a means of performing the various external works of the Church.

REQUISITES FOR APOSTOLATE

The purpose of this inquiry is to analyze the way in which the apostolate of religious groups operates, the people who are involved in both the direction and the accomplishment of functions, and the conditions which affect, positively and negatively the achievement of desired goals. Certain preliminary considerations point to basic prerequisites, that is, to conditions upon which the fulfillment of the apostolic purpose is contingent. In other words, unless the following conditions are established,[2]

---

1. Apostolic Constitution, *Sponsa Christi*, see Gambari, *op. cit.*, p. 89.

one can hardly speak intelligently about the serious pursuit of apostolic goals.

a) The apostolic services which the religious community can provide for the Church and for society must be useful and needed. A group which is performing actions for which there is no demand, or which are merely peripheral, is wasting its time. For an absurd example, a group established for the redemption of slaves in a society where slavery does not exist, or a group that offers to teach hand-weaving in a society where all fabrics are machine-woven, could well turn its attention to needed services. There are, of course, degrees of social need, and the alert community tends to adapt to the greatest needs.

In general, this is not a problem among the dynamic American religious orders. The apostolic services now being rendered by religious communities, especially by the religious Sisters, are highly valued, necessary, useful and in great demand.[3] Everywhere we hear about the shortage of vocations, and the inability of religious superiors to comply with all of the requests made for help. We need merely to mention the great demand for religious teachers to staff the expanding parochial elementary school system throughout the country. To speak in business terminology, it is a "supplier's market."

b) The second prerequisite is to have at hand a willing and competent "work force." The apostolic needs of the society cannot be met unless there are people able and willing to do the work. The conditions of living and of working must provide for the satisfaction of the needs of the members of the religious community, so that they will desire to function cooperatively in and for the group.[4] It will not suffice to say that any dedicated religious person should have the internal spiritual and intellectual resources to put up with a poor work environment and still do a good job.

---

2. These conditions are adapted from the findings of twenty personnel executives and are the result of accumulated experience in business administration. See "The Function and Scope of Personnel Administration," *Personnel,* vol. 24, no. 1, (July, 1947), pp. 5-8.

3. The Holy Father has spoken in the highest praise of these services. "How could the Church in the later and more modern times have fully accomplished her mission without the work of the hundreds of thousands of religious women performed with such great zeal in education and charity? How could she accomplish it in our day?" *Acta Apostolicae Sedis,* vol. 43, (1951), p. 739.

4. F. J. Roethlisberger points out that in order to get cooperation from people "one has to see and understand what is important to them from their point of view. People are curious in that they do not like to be treated as means to someone else's ends; they like to be treated as ends in themselves. To be exclusively concerned with their productivity is to treat them as means to management's ends." Quoted by Pigors and Myers, *op. cit.,* p. 120.

The point here is not merely that "happy workers are productive workers." This may be true, but it is only half the truth. The person has to be allowed, and even encouraged, to become absorbed in the work and to get satisfaction out of it. If there are nervous tensions and even breakdowns, grumblings and dissatisfaction, we can expect that the apostolic functions of the community will be half-done, or done very poorly. The so-called misfits and the shirkers are sometimes persons who are expected to produce more than they are able to in an environment that is not conducive to effective performance.

c) Another prerequisite is the intelligent and effective utilization of the productive means available to the group.[5] This includes human beings and their talents, as well as the spiritual and physical media at the disposal of the community. If required talent is not sufficient and if the people have not been properly trained, there is little that can be said about proper utilization, but the assumption here must be that talent and training have been made available by the higher authorities whose duty it is to supply personnel for the particular apostolic function of the local community.

Obviously then, desired results cannot be obtained if the right tools and materials are not at hand or if the people do not know how to use them. This whole question focuses on the organizational, the so-called structural-functional, aspect of the apostolic group. Here again the task lies with the person who is in charge of the local group. "If she is Superior of a boarding-school or a hospital, she must possess the technical competence needed for the administration of her establishment," [6] and this technical competence includes the ability to supervise professional functionaries.

These three prerequisites for a successfully operating apostolic group cannot be supplied by the rank-and-file members of the group. They are not in themselves a question of obedience, virtue, talent, or activity, on the part of subjects. They are the direct responsibility of the superiors

---

5. Pope Pius XII, in his exhortation to teaching Sisters, said "You wish to serve the cause of Jesus Christ and His Church according to the needs of the modern world. Therefore, it would not be reasonable to persist in usages or ways that impede such service or perhaps even make it impossible." *Acta Apostolicae Sedis,* vol. 43, (1951), p. 742.

6. Paul Phillippe, O.P., "Qualities Necessary for the Superior," *Proceedings* of the 1953 Sister's Institute of Spirituality, (Notre Dame: University of Notre Dame Press, 1954), p. 18. It is widely held principle among experts in the field that the personnel manager must have experience and close knowledge of the "production problems." See Glenn Gardiner, "The Operating Executive and the Personnel Department," in *Personnel Functions and the Line Organization,* American Management Association, Personnel Series No. 121, (1948).

of the religious group, or in some cases, of those outside the group, like bishops or pastors, who control the conditions under which the local superior has to operate.

KINDS OF ACTIVE APOSTOLATE

In this analysis we limit the definition of the active apostolate to that relationship in which organized groups of religious functionaries perform service for the laity. The best-known examples of this are found in the operation of schools and hospitals, and the most numerous groups in these apostolic works are the congregations of religious Sisters. Although we arbitrarily exclude consideration of parish priests at this point, we may note in passing that more than sixteen thousand parishes provide the most frequent, and perhaps the most enduring contact between the official Church and its lay members.[7]

If we omit parishes, as well as the training places for the religious functionary — like seminaries and novitiates — we find that the Church in America operates 14,368 establishments in which the apostolic work of the Church is performed.[8] The following table shows that the overwhelming number (88.5%) of these places are dedicated to education at various levels and of various kinds. These statistics do not show the relative number of people who are served in these establishments. From this point of view, it is obvious that the turnover of patients in general hospitals makes it possible to serve many more people than the statistics may indicate.

TABLE I.—DISTRIBUTION OF ESTABLISHMENTS OF RELIGIOUS ORDERS PERFORMING APOSTOLIC WORKS.

	Number	Percent
Elementary Schools	9,738	67.8
High Schools	2,372	16.5
Colleges and Universities	258	1.8
Schools of Nursing	339	2.4
Hospitals	927	6.5
Homes for the Aged	303	2.1
Orphanages	298	2.0
Protective Institutions	133	0.9
Totals	14,368	100.0

7. See Joseph H. Fichter, *Social Relations in the Urban Parish*, (Chicago: University of Chicago Press, 1954), chap. 10, "Social Roles of the Parish Priest."

8. *The Catholic Directory*, (New York: Kenedy, 1957). These figures are for continental United States only.

If we turn our attention from the establishments to the personnel who staff them, we are immediately struck by the fact that the chief burden of performing these apostolic works lies squarely on the shoulders of the religious Sisters. In the educational field they constitute 86.6 percent of all the religious functionaries who are engaged in teaching,[9] and in the other forms of apostolic work the percentage is even higher. Since this is the case, it may be more fruitful to discuss this question only from the point of view of Sisters' congregations.

TABLE II.—DISTRIBUTION OF FEMALE RELIGIOUS PERSONNEL IN THE PRINCIPAL APOSTOLIC WORKS OF TWENTY-SIX AMERICAN ARCHDIOCESES.[10]

Occupation	Number	Percent
Teaching	43,461	80.7
Hospital Work	6,240	11.6
Orphanages	2,047	3.8
Homes for the Aged	1,394	2.6
Protective Institutions	721	1.3
Totals	53,863	100.0

The significance of these statistics for the apostolate of the Church in America cannot be overemphasized. They prove beyond any doubt that the main contribution of religious orders to the work of the Church is an active, external one. Even though the rules and regulations, and perhaps some of the expressed ideals, of these groups attempt to orient the members to the contemplative, cloistered and monastic form of life, the fact remains that the principal function is a "contact job" with the world.

It is impossible in this social situation to flee the world in the old monastic sense. "The monastic life, as organized in the early middle ages, was essentially contemplative. The search was for God and all links with the world were broken. The monk concerned himself with worldly affairs no longer; he lived in God. No longer having any human interests, he not only renounced marriage, but he renounced everything

---

9. According to the *Catholic Directory* (1957) there were 8,979 priests, 4,418 brothers, 1,135 scholastics, and 94,197 Sisters engaged in full-time teaching.

10. These archdioceses contain 79,609 Sisters, representing forty-nine percent of all Sisters in the United States. Those not included in the above table are in various categories. Some are sick and retired, others are in contemplative orders, and the great majority are in houses of study and formation.

except God. . . . He was preoccupied with nothing, he desired nothing. In the same way, he did what he was told to do; to be able to decide what he would do was of no importance." [11]

The contrast between the hidden, monastic life and the open, apostolic life, has been drawn many times, and it is a problem that the founders of active orders always wrestled with. Men went out even from the early monasteries to do missionary work in the world, and at a latter time new orders made a deliberate adaptation to the needs of their age. This fact is carefully pointed out by the Holy Father. "The legislators of religious orders have usually planned their work, which was then something new, with a view to meeting the needs of or rendering the services required in the Church, neither of which admitted of any delay: consequently they adapted their enterprises to the needs of their time. If you wish to follow the example of your fathers, then do as they did. Study the opinions, the judgments and the customs of your contemporaries among whom you live, and if you there find details which are good and right, then take possession of these precious elements." [12]

GROWTH OF PROFESSIONALISM

Whether we like it or not, the persons involved in these tasks are no longer enacting only a professional religious role; they are forced by the needs which they are attempting to fulfill to become professionals in the particular apostolic roles. They can no longer be well-intentioned amateurs, trusting that their good will and holiness can make up for a lack of training, competence and talent. "A profession is an occupation for which the necessary preliminary training is intellectual in character, involving knowledge and to some extent learning, as distinguished from mere skill; which is pursued largely for others, and not merely for one's self; and in which the financial return is not the accepted measure of success." [13]

The dilettante or the amateur cannot fulfill the role of the professional because he has not been trained to be a professional and cannot

---

11. Jacques LeClercq, *The Religious Vocation,* (New York: Kenedy, 1955), pp. 60-61. He points out that this was the theory and the trend of monastic life. The monk was not concerned with action. "It is obvious that in practice this could be achieved to only a limited extent."

12. Pius XII, Discourse to the Congress on the States of Perfection, December 8, 1950. In line with the Pontiff's advice to study the customs of contemporaries, Abbé Kothen, *op. cit.,* p. 146, says in passing that a superior "should perhaps consult a manual on the psychology of the administration of business affairs."

13. Justice Louis Brandeis, quoted by Paul Pigors and Charles Myers, *Personnel Administration,* (New York: McGraw-Hill, 1947), p. 308.

be expected to have the attitudes of the professional.[14] In most instances he is even blissfully unaware of the requirements of the professional role. The professional apostolic religious functionary is the person who gives his full working time to a career for which he has had some training. He performs the central and essential roles in every organized social group. He is indispensable to both the maintenance of the organization and the achievement of its goals. He bears the brunt of action; he gives direction and integration to the whole system. While it is true that God has the power to raise the foolish to the point where they can confound the wise, it is hardly possible that God wants His dedicated followers to be deliberately foolish or non-professional.

As a result of empirical studies social scientists have analyzed the professional role in the American social system. From these studies and analyses certain general elements have been derived as characteristics of the professional functionary. These studies in the sociology of occupations can perhaps provide for us a reliable comparison between the professional religious functionary and the professionals in other major social groupings.[15]

a) The first characteristic has been called *functional specificity,* which means that there is a clearly defined activity or set of activities belonging only to this role. In relation to other roles, and indeed to other persons outside his occupation, the authority of the person is limited to a particular technically defined area. The role of teacher, of nurse, of social worker, is not "diffused" in various directions. It is specified by known limitations and is specialized by its content. From this point of view, the apostolic role of the religious reflects a professionalism that is quite distinct from the professional aspects of the "purely" religious role.

b) The second characteristic of the professional is that of *technical competence.* The individual has the training, knowledge and abilities necessary to perform the function successfully. He is not a "bungler." The more difficult the function the rarer is high proficiency in its performance. Here again, the religious functionary is often in competition with others in secular groupings, who perform as a key occupational role that which the religious enacts as a subsidiary role. The Holy Father has insisted that this technical competence of the religious must be at

14. See the development of this point in "How Can Sociology Aid the Vocation Apostolate?" *Proceedings* of the Tenth Annual Vocation Institute, (Notre Dame: University of Notre Dame Press, 1957), pp. 55-67.

15. See Talcott Parsons, "The Professions and Social Structure,"*Essays in Sociological Theory,* revised ed., (Glencoe: Free Press, 1954), pp. 34-49; also *ibid.,* "A Sociologist Looks at the Legal Profession," pp. 370-385.

least equal to the best of the contemporary specialists in secular areas.[16]

c) The next mark of the professional is that he is *collectivity-oriented* rather than self-oriented. His role is meant to be motivated by disinterested service rather than by self-interested profit. This is why the lawyer, the physician, the teacher, whose main reason for existing is the service of others, are called professional people in contrast to the businessman. From the point of view of service to others, the religious functionary may well be called the most professional person in the world. In the apostolic role he has dedicated himself to God precisely by giving himself to the ministry of man. Ideally, then, he is not self-motivated or self-oriented.[17]

d) Another characteristic of the professional is that he enacts what may be called a *universalistic role*. This means that his service is open to all comers who are in need of it. From the point of view of the client, the emphasis here is on the needs of people and not on the kind of people who are in need. If we translate this into spiritual terms, we may say that the charity of the servant of God is expressed in the universal service of God's people. The concrete conditions of time and space and human endurance put limitations on the universalism, but the role nonetheless remains typically universalistic.

e) Finally, the professional role is marked by *affective neutrality,* which means that emotional involvement has no place in the strictly professional performance.[18] He does not give service only to those he likes, nor does he give them better service. The measure of his professionalism in this regard is not his affection for his beneficiaries, but their need for his service and his ability to render this service. In the everyday situation probably the most that can be expected is that the professional's fondness or lack of fondness for people must not be allowed to interfere with the performance of his role.

HANDLING THE PROFESSIONAL

If our analysis has been correct up to this point we must probably

---

16. Although urging the nursing Sisters to equal, and even surpass, in technical advantages those who perform the same service out of humanitarianism or pay, the Holy Father points out that "where our religious women, deeply imbued with the vital spirit of their institutes and daily prepared for the love of Christ to lay down their lives for the sick, perform their labors, a different atmosphere prevails, in which virtue works wonders that technical aids and medical skill alone are powerless to accomplish." Address to Religious Men. December 8, 1950.

17. See Charles Corcoran, C.S.C., "The Apostolate as a Means of Sanctification," *Proceedings* of the 1957 Sisters' Institute of Spirituality, (Notre Dame: University of Notre Dame Press, 1958), especially pp. 179-184, "The Great Obstacle, Selfishness."

18. In the literature of spirituality this characteristic is called "detachment."

reach the conclusion that the active apostolic role of the American religious functionary is something quite new in the history of the Church. We must remember that this person is the product of a relatively unique culture, and that his effective work must be done among people who are also acculturated on the American scene. It appears, therefore, that modes of authority, geared to other cultures and another age can no longer maximize the effectiveness of the religious apostolate.[19] People who are performing professional functions cannot produce efficiently if they are handled like school children or unskilled workers.

As a result of field research in productive organizations social scientists have derived a set of simple formulae that appear easily translatable to the operation of active religious communities. These generalizations are not meant to be guides in the training or formation of religious persons, but only in the practical management of the group made up of competent and trained persons. The following points are the result of realistic experience during World War II, when "getting results" was a vital national issue. These leadership principles were taught to over four hundred thousand supervisors by the War Manpower Commission between February, 1943 and February, 1945.[20]

a) People must be *treated as responsible individuals*. If they cannot be treated in this way they do not belong in the position they occupy and have probably never been given the training that would fit them for that position. The assumption here is that the expert professional "knows his business," and that he has the experience and maturity to fulfill its demands. Lack of trust in a subject's ability and accountability is probably the first defect in an incompetent leader.[21] It is probably also the principal reason why ordinarily efficient people slack off in their work and less efficient people become indifferent and slipshod in their efforts.

b) The superior must appoint the individual to the *position where his abilities are of most use*. This means that the functionary should be allowed and encouraged to do the things that he is best able to do. It is a standing complaint in large organizations — and the military is most

---

19. This can be said only if there is an assumption that the traditional procedural orientation makes way for an emphasis on professionalism.

20. See Paul Pigors and Charles Myers, *Personnel Administration*, (New York: McGraw-Hill, 1947), pp. 498-499. See also Edward C. Bursk, ed., *Human Relations for Management*, (New York: Harper, 1956), chap. 2, by Elizabeth and Francis Jennings, "Making Human Relations Work."

21. "The regulations which date from previous centuries often seem to be inspired by a considerable distrust of the religious themselves. They give the impression of being designed for vocations which have developed in a hothouse, sheltered from human contacts, and need protection if they are to survive." See Jacques LeClercq, *op. cit.*, p. 75.

often cited as the worst example — that talent is wasted by being either misplaced or poorly employed. In religious communities the excuse is often given that shortage of personnel forces the shifting of people to jobs in which they have little competence, but this excuse can be traced back directly to the administrators who took on functions that their community was not prepared to fulfill. A man makes his best contribution to the common goals in a spot where he can do his best work.[22] It is the responsibility of superiors to watch for talent that is lying fallow, and also to remove obstacles that hinder a man who is willing and able to produce.

c) The alert superior is never afraid to *give credit* to those who deserve it. This does not mean an occasional "slap on the back" or a word of general encouragement. It means watching for extra or unusual performance, and it implies that the superior has a genuine understanding of the value of the work that is being performed. Perhaps nothing can more quickly kill the spirit of zealous initiative, out of which unusual performance springs, than the failure of the superior to recognize the value of the work. What can be said of the superior who, deliberately or indeliberately, appears to belittle the successful efforts of his subjects? It is certainly no merit of the superior if in this case the subject happens to possess an extraordinary degree of humility and zeal that permits him to continue doing excellent work.[23] In most cases this probably should not be expected.

d) Closely allied with this point is the guiding principle that the superior should *let each person know how he is getting along.* In religious communities this is the correlative of the periodic conference of the subject with the provincial, which in many instances appears either to have an exclusively moral connotation or is treated in a much too hasty fashion. Insofar as the superior understands the particular function that is being performed — and this is seldom the case in highly specialized professional roles — he ought to be able to apprize the functionary of "where he stands." The least that can be expected of the local superior is that he have a general idea of the way in which the

---

22. Rahner, *op. cit.*, p. 297, remarks that "authority, even in religious orders, in practice needs, calls for, and puts to use the initiative of subjects. Even in the abstract, there can be no *absolute* ruler and director of it. Independently of authority there exist initial sparkings of forces which cannot be controlled by authority. Because this is so and cannot be otherwise, it also *should* be so."

23. It may be helpful to reread the celebrated second chapter of Claude Aquaviva's *Industriae,* where he gives practical advice to superiors concerning "Effective Governing." See the English version under this title in the *Review for Religious,* vol. 14, (September, 1955), pp. 235-240.

particular function of the subject fits into the external apostolic goal of the community itself. Of course, the assumption throughout this point is that the superior has both interest in and knowledge of what the subjects are doing.[24]

e) A final principle of effective leadership is the giving of open *information concerning prospective changes*. This implies that the superior has confidence in both the work and the worker, and that he will give advance notice of changes that will affect the subject's role.[25] If possible, the superior should give an adequate explanation of the reasons why the changes are being made and attempt to get cooperative acceptance of the changes.[26] This is particularly necessary in the case of highly specialized functionaries who, because of their initiative and responsibility and because of their dedication to the work, almost necessarily have long-range plans of their own. Perhaps it is true to say that no one is indispensable, and while this may be said of the person performing the function it cannot be said of the function itself if the group is to continue successfully towards its apostolic goal.

---

24. This and the following point are aspects of the communication system of the organization. For a brief discussion of it, see William Finlay, A. Q. Sartain, Willis Tate, *Human Behavior in Industry*, (New York: McGraw-Hill, 1954), chap. 9, "Communication, A Major Function of Management."

25. Archbishop Roberts, *op. cit.*, p. 4, goes so far as to say that "it is humanly impossible to exercise authority without consulting the governed. To deny this is to make nonsense of obedience."

26. "The modern man is quite willing to obey, but he wants to know why: his resistance to obedience comes from his difficulty in grasping what the superior expects of him." Victor de la Vierge, O.C.D., "Applications of the Principle of Adaptation," in Albert Plé, O.P., ed., *op. cit.*, (Westminster: Newman Press, 1954), p. 267.

VI

The Authority of Function

Although both the apprentice and the master-workman are members of the same social organization and subject to the same superior, authority itself is not exercised in the same way toward both of them. A recruit in a boot camp and a Lieutenant Colonel in the General Staff are both subject to the Commander-in-Chief of the Armies, but it would be absurd to suggest that both respond, or are expected to respond, to their superior in the same way. These illustrations can be carried over also to the difference in the way authority is exercised toward a novice or a religious in his formative years and toward an adult trained functionary in the religious community.

The point to be made here is not that authority is mitigated as a subject grows older in the religious life, or that the more mature religious person relaxes and takes less seriously the need for authority. Either or both of these may be true in some instances but this view of the situation misses completely the question of authority as exercised toward the competent and professional religious functionary. As long as the person is in the process of religious formation, or as long as his way of life is strictly contemplative, there may be a need for devices which fortify the habit of obedience. We leave it to the ascetical theologian to decide whether corpselike obedience and impossible commands (that can be obeyed only through miraculous intervention; therefore, only by God) are useful tools in the development of today's religious apostles.[1]

The professional functions of active apostolic religious communities in modern America cannot be performed either by corpses or by apprentices in the religious life. The nursing Sister who is assigned by obedience to the operating room of a hospital cannot stop and phone her

---

1. Archbishop Robert, *op. cit.,* p. 10, says that St. Ignatius probably would not have used the cadaver analogy if he had foreseen the way in which the antagonists of the Church would employ it. Rahner, *op. cit.,* p. 304, remarks that "obedience is not at all to be conceived as the heroic (or almost foolhardy) concession of a *carte blanche* to a superior, so that the religious simply does not do his own will, either because this is always pleasing and hence its renunciation especially difficult, or because it is fraught with danger and hence to be avoided."

superior every time a decision must be made about which instrument to hand the surgeon. The teaching Sister who has been assigned by her superior to instruct a class of children cannot delay the multitude of small decisions required of her until they have been cleared with the superior. This seems so obvious that it hardly needs restatement, but this illustration contains a most significant insight into the functioning of authority.

These religious functionaries are not responsible only to their superiors or to their clients, patients, or charges. They are specifically responsible to the demands of the professional function itself. "There are old tales of holy religious whose religious work was done all wrong, because their thoughts were entirely on God; there was the cook who produced inedible food, because his mind was absent with God, and the monk, who having to dig over a bed of vegetables, dug up the plants with the earth, because he was not thinking of how his work should be done." [2] One may admire the other-worldliness of these ancient monks, but one can hardly commend them for an intelligent job well-done, nor could one tolerate them for a moment in the active religious apostolate.

What we are saying here is that the work itself demands obedience of the worker, but it would be an error of the first magnitude to suggest that there is an inherent conflict between the authority of the superior and the authority of the function. [3] We are speaking here of the intelligent professional whose work demands intelligent cooperation, not of the assembly-line worker whose job is repetitive and almost automatic and whose thinking has been done for him by the machine-design engineers. Once the religious subject has been assigned to a professional role in the religious community his actions and decisions must be shaped by the demands of the role. In this sense, the function itself "has authority" over the functionary; and the superior who does not understand this or who interferes with it is acting unintelligently. He is not aware of the logical operation of the modern apostolate, and is probably thinking of work and authority in the old-fashioned monastic sense.

It is precisely here that the whole problem of bureaucracy and professionalism again comes to the fore. Both forms of organization, together

---

2. See Jacques LeClercq, *The Religious Vocation,* (Kenedy: New York, 1955), p. 135.

3. The point here is that the knowledgeable professional is forced to follow the *truth* contained in the role he performs and is unable by sheer force of will to embrace a contrary and erroneous opinion of his superior. This point is worthy of deep reflection in the present context and is excellently made by Augustine G. Ellard, S.J., "A Rational Approach to Intellectual Obedience," *Review for Religious,* vol. 14, (September, 1955), pp. 261-265.

with the communal order of social relations, are present in the normal active religious community. The fact that the function itself "contains" authority and thus demands obedience of the functionary, does not supply the total solution to this problem. It is only one element — an extremely important one — in a whole series of items that must be taken into consideration. One may flippantly suggest that the religious community that is unwilling to be obedient to the "demands of the job" would do well to channel its energies into some other form of God's service. This is, of course, sheer escapism and is not consonant with the goals of active apostolic groups.

CONCEPTIONS OF WORK

Underlying the confusion that seems to surround the distinction between authority of function and authority of person appears to an outmoded conception of work itself as a human activity. In this conception work is considered basically unpleasant, a kind of necessary evil that man must endure as a consequence of his fallen nature. It is punishment for sins, a form of penance we have to go through here on earth "in the sweat of our brows" in order to reach our eternal salvation. The mental and physical effort involved in work is thought of in terms of distasteful drudgery. People who held this conception of work are subconsciously disquieted, and perhaps even have feelings of guilt, because human intelligence and ingenuity have been able to mechanize work and thus to take the heaviest burdens off the backs of labor.

A quite different conception of work is that of an activity that is basically satisfying to the human being.[4] In this sense the worker gets a feeling of accomplishment and fulfillment, because he is able to express himself, to employ his positive talents, and to satisfy his creative needs. This does not mean that work is an end in itself, but that it serves more than a penitential purpose. It satisfies not only the needs of other people by producing goods and services for them, and not only the needs of the worker by providing income for the necessities of life; but above all it satisfies the individual's need for human and meaningful action.

We must be careful not to draw a sharp line between these two conceptions of work as though they were totally disconnected. The distinction here is one of attitude and emphasis. No one knows better than the dedicated professional that work still remains work even when it is sat-

---

4. This twofold conception of work is developed by F. J. Roethlisberger, "The Human Equation in Employee Productivity," in Pigors and Myers, editors, *Readings in Personnel Administration*, (New York: McGraw-Hill, 1952), pp. 114-115.

isfying, successful and meaningful. The teacher and the nurse find some aspects of their work less satisfying than other aspects. Although mechanical technics and improved methods have lightened the burden of work even in these professions there still remain functional components of the role that require routine endurance and fidelity to details. Nevertheless, the psychological element of "enjoying one's work" is an immeasurable contribution toward the competent performance of the work.[5]

Another caution must be made at this point, and this concerns the so-called secularization of work. Although we are here analyzing work from a sociological point of view, the fact remains that the labors of the religious functionary are imbued with supernatural ideals. Briefs point out that "through long centuries of Christian civilization transcendent values and the supernatural destiny of man ennobled even the most humble type of work. Labor had its place in the hierarchy of values because it had its meaning in the education and sanctification of man." The Christian philosophy of labor implied "the elevation of the worker as a person, who through his work met his needs and realized the ultimate welfare of his soul." [6] Even on this religious level of human endeavor, however, it is possible to recognize both the penitential and the creative attitudes toward work.

Since very few workers are completely independent, the attitude that their superiors have toward work will necessarily affect them. The religious superior is a good case in point here because the exercise of his authority can immediately affect his subjects. The superior who has the first concept of work ordinarily makes two practical judgments in relation to his subjects. The first is that since work is simply a means to salvation, one job is the same as another. It does not matter what the subject does so long as he does what he is told, and there must be no hesitancy in jumping from one kind of work to another. Since the superior is a kindly and sympathetic person, however, he becomes solicitous about overwork on the part of his subjects. After all, since work is hard and unpleasant he does not want to be guilty of condemning his subjects to too much of it.[7] He knows about nervous breakdowns and he thinks they all come from overwork.

---

5. There exists a whole literature on the theology of work which throws light on this question for the religious functionary.

6. Goetz A. Briefs, *The Proletariat*, (New York: McGraw-Hill, 1937), pp. 276-277.

7. It is a well-known fact that the successful career man in secular pursuits is a man of energy, drive and hard work. Members of religious communities are probably never called upon to "keep up a pace" of this kind. Yet Ignatius Loyola thought that the love of God could motivate us even better than the way worldly people are motivated by non-supernatural incentives.

The superior who thinks of work in the second conception, as that of a satisfying human activity, also has his scruples.[8] In this case he is worried that success may make his subjects proud, especially if they are in highly specialized professional fields where achievement wins the plaudits of the larger society. Furthermore, the religious superior with this view of work is afraid also of what is sometimes called the "heresy of action." He fears that the subject may become so immersed in his work that he becomes "intoxicated with action in a purely natural way." [9] Here again, the superior knows of sad cases of intractable religious subjects and he thinks that they all come from the fact that the individual enjoyed his work too much and had too much success with it.

A great deal could be said at this point — and usually is — about the need for humility, charity and personal sanctification on the part of the subject. We are, however, focusing our attention upon the superior and upon the exercise of his authority toward hard-working, intelligent and apostolic religious functionaries. How does his concept of apostolic work affect his direction of subjects? Perhaps the answer lies back in the period of spiritual formation and training when the subject was imbued with a "divine indifference" or disinterestedness towards the active apostolate and was constantly warned against the "dangers" of enjoying work and becoming too immersed in it. If the basic problem does lie in this direction, it is mainly the problem of the superior responsible for the formation of young religious.

The superior who ignores, tones down, or fears the professional success of his subjects as individuals, must be in a dilemmatic position when he prays God to bless (that is, bring success to) the apostolic efforts of the religious community as a whole. Given the grace of God and the intelligent good will of the religious members, the apostolic success of the community is measured by the individual achievement of its functionaries. Insofar as we can measure these items on a natural level (and we must allow God to do the supernatural measurement) the apostolic results achieved are those of the holy and competent people who put in the effort, and not of the religious community *in vacuo*. The superior who gets in the way of his hard-working subjects, whether through ignorance or scrupulosity, is interfering with the apostolic function of his community. He is frustrating the expectations of the Church in regard to his community.

---

8. "The anxiety of those responsible for training these young people is very real when they see subjects, often very valuable ones, enter the novitiate full of enthusiasm and there as a result of strain, restlessness and anxiety, gradually lose all that is best in them." Victor de la Vierge, O.C.D., *op. cit.*, p. 245.

9. See Jacques LeClercq, *op. cit.*, p. 168.

Formation of Professionals

Many of the problem areas of the relationship between the religious superior and the adult religious subject current in the active apostolic communities appear to have their source in the training ground of novitiates and houses of study. It is in these places where the young American is formed, or reformed, according to the model in the mind of the superior. It is to be supposed that the people in charge of these places do have a fairly clear mental image of the kind of human product they are molding, and that they are employing what they consider the proper means to this end. What is this mental image of the future religious functionary, and what are these means?

It will be recalled that one of the characteristics differentiating the professional from the non-professional is that the latter is typically oriented to self-interest and the former to service of others. Obviously, these characteristics are never found in "pure type," a professional may be selfish and a non-professional may be unselfish, but the orientation is not so much in the personal qualities as in the role the person enacts. The typical professional role is pointed toward the service of others, while in the non-professional role — like that of the businessman — the profit motive is not only considered permissible but often laudable.

Now a striking analogy is apparent here when we analyze the formation of persons within a religious community. The monastic ideals of personal sanctification, formulated at a time when the role to be attained was that of the contemplative religious, still seem to persist in some novitiates and seminaries. The books on spirituality, which are assigned reading for the neophyte, often reflect ideals of individual perfection. They suggest that retirement from the world is desirable, that contact with the world may be a soiling experience, and that the aspirant to sanctity should not only renounce, but also denounce, the world.

We are talking here of apparent emphases in training, and of general attitudes that the trainee takes away from this program. The experts in asceticism tell us, of course, that sanctity cannot be so neatly divided into personal and social, and the Scriptures tell us that that person is a liar who says that he loves God but does not love his neighbor. Therefore, even if the sole purpose of the religious community were the personal sanctification of the individual member it would necessarily include an abiding concern for the salvation of others. The active, apostolic communities of religious in America are definitely committed to "work for others" and the orientation of their members demands a clearer concept of social morality.

The problem seems to lie in the common notion that training in personal perfection is one thing and professional preparation for the apostolic role is another thing. We need not belabor the obvious point that holiness does not take the place of pedagogical talent, or that a successful teacher is not necessarily a holy person.[10] The point is that the apostolic orientation in spiritual development is towards the service (salvation) of others just as the professional orientation in technical development is towards the service of others. Exclusive concentration on self-perfection is almost necessarily a block to successful external apostolic performance.

In this limited concept of sanctity, personal perfection is supposed to spill over into charity towards others. The notion contained in it seems to say that a person is unable to help others to holiness unless he is himself already at an advanced stage of holiness. The central problem here lies in the supposition that the apostolic function will somehow *automatically* occur when individual sanctity has been taken care of, and *only* as long as one constantly focuses his efforts on his own perfection. Without being disrespectful to those who promote such notions, one may suggest the parallel among dedicated commercial people who say that what is good for their business is good for their country.

The contrast between self-centered and social-centered spirituality in the training of future religious functionaries is accentuated even further when we consider two basic characteristics of the professional role: functional specificity and technical competence.[11] If the novice or seminarian is not given an apostolic perspective in his early years we can expect that he will become a spiritual jack-of-all-trades. In attempting obediently to fit in wherever the superior places him, we find him shifting from one place to another and fitting in none of them. He is likely to be a second-rate performer who is not himself satisfied and who satisfies neither his local superior, his companions or the people he is meant to serve.

We have seen also that the enactment of the professional role in any

---

10. It is a commonplace observation that expert scholar of the law may himself be a law-breaker and that a physician does not always follow his own counsel. Christ Himself recognized the competence of the scribes and pharisees who sat on the chair of Moses, but who were not to be imitated.

11. "The counsels of perfection are not the freezing point of human endeavor and ingenuity." "The religious life must not be the cradle of ineptitude." Pius XII has indicated that "the modern apostolate requires one who can face boldly the gigantic tasks of our age, one able to meet its dangers, overcome its spiritual destitution, competent to think for himself, and formed to maturity of judgment." John F. Gallen, S.J., "Renovation and Adaptation," *Review for Religious*, vol. 14, (November, 1955), pp. 293-318.

social system requires initiative and responsibility. These two qualities are the resultant of long and careful training and we cannot expect them to appear by fiat of the superior, nor do they somehow rub off even on the best-intentioned person merely by virtue of appointment to a specific role. A certain childishness can be detected in some adult religious persons, a failure to grasp the importance of work and to make the adaptations that every dynamic professional role requires. A training program that sets out deliberately to keep a person in a perpetual state of childlike dependence cannot possibly develop a person of initiative and responsibility.[12]

AUTHORITY AND DECISION

Since the person in authority is the one who "gives orders" there is a common misapprehension that making decisions and giving orders are somehow synonymous. The fact is, of course, that the making of decisions is a much broader area of action than is the exercise of authority. People have to make personal decisions all the time, and no religious can escape this under the pretext of having made "one grand and all embracing" decision at the time of taking vows. This kind of thinking is at best a rationalization for irresponsibility on the part of the religious subject, and at worst a mockery of the whole process of obedience.

Aside from personal decisions, which may involve highly technical matters in which the professional religious functionary is competent, there are also important organizational decisions — and these are ordinarily considered the responsibility of management. The fact is, however, that most of the activity involved in these organization decisions is not strictly a part of the function of authority. Roughly, this activity may be divided into four logical steps: (a) the recognition of the problem; (b) the analysis of alternatives; (c) the choice of one of the alternatives; and (d) the executive order that this choice should be put into effect.

It is only in the last step that authority is called into play. All three preceding steps are preliminary to the exercise of authority, and in the

---

12. One Provincial withdrew a brilliant young nun from graduate studies because "she showed herself entirely too efficient in arranging her own classes, conferring with professors and making her own educational plans." This nun was one of the best college teachers in the order, but she was sent to an obscure high school "until she learned that religious obedience took precedence over all intellectual pursuit." See Sister Bertrande Meyers, *The Education of Sisters*, (New York: Sheed and Ward, 1941), p. 85. For a contrast to this, see the remarks of John J. Lazarsky on "Professional and Human Training," in *Proceedings, op. cit.*, pp. 308-317.

largest organizations they are often performed by consultants and experts who are themselves not invested with the power to give orders.[13] This is not a discovery of social science, but it appears to have the force of discovery in religious communities where the superior's council has been operating in a perfunctory manner, or where the superior still thinks it is possible to handle all management problems personally. The very purpose of the council, or advisory board, is to provide the preliminary foundations upon which the superior can finally make the decision.

Canonists point out the difference between the General Chapter, which has authority over the Superior General, and the General Council, over which the Superior General has authority.[14] The members of the council do not share in the authority of the superior from the point of view of decision-making, but the very purpose of their office is to share in the responsibilities of management. In a simple culture where the apostolic works of the religious community were relatively routinized and demanded little specialization, and in internal problem areas which were foreseen by the prescriptions of the institute, the preliminary steps to decision probably required little consultation. The council members acted mainly as a brake on the superior's ambitions, and contributed to the morale of the community.

All of this has changed in a complex culture where the apostolic works of religious communities are highly institutionalized by criteria and practices that originate outside the traditional religious instituton. Because of this socio-cultural change there are several important reasons why the management function preliminary to the giving of orders must be shared by the superior. The first reason is that no superior can possibly know enough to perform adequately all of the management functions. "Every religious superior has many subjects who necessarily possess a knowledge of science, of pastoral functioning, of current affairs, which the superior (who can be a specialist himself in only a single limited field) cannot possess." For this reason, "the advisors, usually provided for superiors by the constitutions of an order, today in many ways possess an utterly new and more urgent function than in former times." [15]

---

13. See Chester I. Bernard, *The Functions of the Executive*, (Cambridge: Harvard University Press, 1945), chap. 13, "The Environment of Decision." His theory of authority is controversial, but his experiences and analysis of administration are an invaluable contribution to this field. See especially his discussion of executive functions, processes and responsibilities, pp. 215-284.

14. Gambari, *op. cit.*, pp. 153-154. See also *Religious Sisters*, (Westminster: Newman Press, 1954), P. Bergh, S.J., part iii, chap. 4, "Government in Practice."

15. Rahner, *op. cit.*, p. 294.

The second reason is that organizational decisions, as contrasted to personal decisions, have far-reaching effects in both time and personnel. This is particularly true in the active external apostolate which touches not only the functionaries within the organization but especially the lay Catholics in the diocese and even the total secular community. Unwise decisions, made in the name of prudence but with practically no knowledge of social and cultural conditions, can seriously diminish, and even directly hinder, the effective performance of the apostolate. These errors could be avoided through preliminary consultation with subjects who are experts.

The third reason is that group morale is strengthened, and effective production is increased, by expanding the area of responsible involvement of the religious subjects. This is predicated not only on the hypothesis that men perform better the functions for which they are responsible by previous approval, but also on the empirical demonstration that this actually works in social organizations. Willing workers always follow better the good directions they understand than the ones they do not understand; and their understanding is immeasurably improved by contributions of knowledge they have made prior to the decision.

It must be clearly pointed out that this analysis is neither an impingement on religious authority nor a species of democratization of the religious community. Setting up concrete and objective methods of procedure in the search for needed knowledge is a logical step prior to any decision, personal or organizational. It is not in itself a function of authority. In many cases of religious communities it is probable that the members of the council do not themselves possess the necessary knowledge and expertness. There is nothing to prevent the superior from going directly to those members of the community who do possess such qualifications. Indeed, it may be argued that the superior has an obligation to do so.

APOSTOLATE AND CULTURE

The apostolic community finds itself in a peculiar position in relation to the American culture in which it operates. It is the representative of a Church which has the reputation of being weighed down with traditionalism and conservatism. Its patterns of behavior and its ideals are interpreted by many Americans, even by Catholics, as stable, solidly anchored, unchanging and unchangeable. Yet this is the group that is being asked by the Holy Father to become a dynamic and penetrating force for change in the total culture.[16] An instrument that has been

16. To the Jesuit General Pope Pius XII wrote: "The new times in which

forged over centuries of experience and that has been used in relatively the same way in many different places is to be reforged in the fire of new needs and new experiences. The religious community is asked not only to make internal adaptations but to apply itself seriously to the gigantic task of reforming the culture in which it exists.

One authority writes that "risks" are involved in this whole process of adaptation, but adds that "the giving or restoring of life always involved risks. The saints risked everything. They knew how to lose their lives and find them again made rich in faith, hope and charity. . . .We might have to sacrifice our peace and quiet which, after all, may not be very spiritual, but if we do not show ourselves today real sons of God in spirit and in truth, real brothers of our brothers, what right shall we have even to exist tomorrow?" [17]

The rational approach to institutional reform is probably not well understood because the influence of the institutional environment on human behavior is not clearly recognized. In a large, complex and specialized society such as ours the pressure towards conformity tends to standardize and routinize the patterns of behavior, and to lessen the likelihood that the individual can successfully contravene the mores. Without gainsaying personal accountability or the strength of divine grace, we can still appreciate the fact that people are not only the creatures of their culture but most of them continue to follow the institutionalized behavior their culture expects of them.

In order to effect a wide-scale reform of personal attitudes as well as of folkways and mores the primary attack has to be on the institutions that form these attitudes and patterns. This is what institutional reform means. The socially accepted and consecrated ways of men in the pursuit of social goals have to be questioned, analyzed, challenged and changed. We have seen some remarkable instances of this reform in recent years within the framework of the Church itself. Perhaps the clearest examples are those of liturgical reform and the changes in the Communion fast. Some people who were "set in their ways" (that is, strongly institutionalized in another system) found it difficult to accept these innovations. Some are still disquieted by them and resist them as evidence of sheer laxity.

we live certainly demand, also in spiritual matters, new undertakings, new works and aids by which we can aptly meet the changed and increasing needs of our age." *Acta Apostolicae Sedis*, vol. 32, (1940), p. 295; and to the General of the Society of Mary: "You are called upon . . . to show yourselves equal to the needs of the times and to undertake courageously all forms of the apostolate introduced by the present age." *Ibid.*, vol. 41, (1949), p. 592.

17. Victor de la Vierge, O.C.D., in Albert Plé, O.P., ed., *Religious Sisters*, (Westminster: Newman Press, 1954), pp. 266, 279.

Now the apostolic task of the religious community — as contrasted to the personal task of helping each individual soul — must be pointed ultimately at the reformation of the major institutions of the culture. This is a question different from that of the internal adaptation of the religious community itself. Often enough, adaptation is promoted in order to "meet modern needs" and these needs are interpreted in things like Sisters driving automobiles or seminarians using typewriters. These internal changes may indeed assist the apostolic workers to do a better job, but we must also ask what they are trying to do by means of "doing a better job." The answer is that they are trying to change the forms of the culture, to Christianize the institutions.

It ought to be clear in all that has been said up to now that the key figure in this tremendous apostolic task of cultural reformation is the religious superior. From one point of view he and his counselors bear the brunt of the responsibility. In the last analysis it is always the top officers of any social organization who can do the most to institute change, and also the most to hinder change. Who, if not they, should be the most zealous in improving the exercise of authority, in revamping the mode of internal community organization, in instituting better ways of training the professional apostle, in encouraging the active, front-line workers to excellent performance?

THE ASCETICAL ASPECTS

OF

THE ROLE OF AUTHORITY IN THE ADAPTATION OF THE RELIGIOUS COMMUNITY FOR THE APOSTOLATE

Reverend Louis J. Putz, C.S.C.

I

The Problem of Adjusting Religious Life and the Apostolate

What would the Catholic Church in this country be without its schools, without its hospitals, its social agencies, old folks homes, orphanages, without the catechetical and mission stations? Now almost all of these are manned by our Sister congregations under their immediate direction and supervision. These are our modern apostolates. When we think that almost all the Sister force is engaged in this wide network of apostolate, it is entirely appropriate that we ask ourselves some important questions concerning the relationship between our spiritual life and the apostolate.

The apostolates are a full-time occupation, whether it be teaching, hospital work or social work. These apostolates are often in competition with their counterparts in the secular fields. The standards are most often set by institutions and a society that is not concerned with the obligations of religious life. We are asking ourselves this week what precisely is the place of the apostolate in the life of religious, whether our religious obligations are a help or a hindrance, whether the apostolate is in conflict with the religious obligations, whether an adaptation is necessary to streamline our religious obligations with the demands of our apostolic life.

We are not advocating that we curtail either the apostolate or the religious life. We want to see their mutual relations in order to integrate our life with our apostolic responsibilities. Ideally there should be no dichotomy, no rub between the two. If there is incompatibility, we want to know whence this arises. Could it come from a religious pattern that is not realistic, not in conformity with the demands of modern society?

In this conference we shall determine what the ideal of the religious life and of the apostolate is. We shall find that the goal of both is the same. In the second conference we shall look historically at the development of asceticism throughout the history of religious life. Then we shall call for a spirituality of action. A fourth talk will concern itself with the social dimension of apostolic asceticism and in the final talk we want to suggest as a solution the need to move in the rhythm of the Church.

I. THE IDEAL OF RELIGIOUS LIFE AND OF THE APOSTOLATE ARE THE SAME: UNION WITH GOD

I say union with God designedly because to speak of love of God and love of neighbor would indicate two distinct movements, whereas love of God and love of neighbor, in Our Lord's use of the term is one and the same love. You recall the lawyer in the Gospel asking Our Lord, "What is the first and greatest commandment of the law?" And Our Lord asked in return what was written in the law and the Prophets. "Thou shalt love the Lord thy God with thy whole mind, heart, soul, will and strength and the second commandment was like the first, Love thy neighbor as thyself." Love of neighbor is our concrete way of expressing our love for God. St. John says: "How can he say that he loves God when he hates his neighbor. For how can one love God whom he does not see, when he does not love his neighbor whom he does see" (I John 5:20). It is when we see God in our neighbor that we truly love God.

It is so easy to lose this ideal and to shift the emphasis from union with God which is charity, to pious attitudes, or religious practices. When this happens, then we are only one step removed from formalism or legalism, which the Holy Father defined in his recent radio talk to contemplative religious as "the temptation to adhere to the letter of the law without fully accepting its spirit." Religious acts or practices, when they are purely external, can give the appearance of religion, of union with God, without necessarily having God as the real object, but self-interest or self-glorification, as it happened in the case of the

Pharisees, whom Our Lord took to task for their deceitful formalism. The same formalism can take over in our lives when we follow the pattern of rules and regulations and exercises of piety without putting a soul into them. They might be a subtle cover-up for laziness, comfort-seeking, when demands are made on our time and energy. The priest and the Levite of the Gospel incident were returning from the temple service to answer the call of duty at home. Yet in the very act of going from one duty to another, they omitted a greater duty, that of coming to the rescue of their compatriot who was in dire need of help. The Samaritan, who might have been more excusable on the grounds of his nationality, which the Jews despised, was nevertheless neighbor to the one overtaken by robbers.

Our Lord's great preoccupation during his public preaching was to put a soul into the external emphasis of the Jewish law. "It was said to them of old, thou shalt not kill, but I say to you, do not hate your neighbor" (Matt. 5:20). "It was said to them of old, do not foreswear thyself, but I say to you do not swear at all, but let your speech be yea, yea" (Matt. 5:33). In other words, be frank and open and truthful without artifice. "It was said to them of old, thou shalt love thy neighbor and hate thy enemy, but I say to you, love thy enemy, love those who think evil of you and calumniate you" (Matt. 5:17). And later in the same Sermon on the Mount, "When you give alms, don't blow the trumpet to call attention to your deed, but let not your right hand know what your left hand does. And when you fast, do not put on a long face as the hypocrites do who make a display of their fasting, but anoint your face yourself and be gay. And when you pray, do not pray in public, but enter your chamber and pray to the Father in secret and He who seeth in secret will reward you" (Matt. 6:2 ff.). In all this it appears that Christ wanted to put a soul into the law and interior spiritual orientation to external behavior. Union with God is established not by external acts alone, whether of prayer or of penance or almsgiving, but by the orientation that we give to these acts.

II. RESPONSIBILITY OF SUPERIORS TO ADJUST THE PATTERN OF RELIGIOUS OBSERVANCE TO APOSTOLIC COMMITMENTS

While our whole life must be orientated to union with God by the proper internal disposition which should be guaranteed by the proper use of the exercises of piety, it is nevertheless the function of authority not merely to enforce a set of rules and regulations which could very easily be a mere cover-up for achieving uniformity of conduct and an appearance of regularity without any soul or spirit to go along with it, but to order the common life in a way that it help in the performance of our duty of state in life. If, for example, teaching and prefecting is my full-time occupation, it is obvious that the religious pattern of life and community living must be geared to facilitate my task that has been assigned to me by obedience. Normally, there should be no dichotomy, no tension, at least no constant tension between my apostolic work and my religious obligations. It is the responsibility of authority on all levels of government, local, provincial and general administration, to guide the welfare of religious by guiding the common good with respect for the destiny of each religious. The individual religious is of greater value than the community or any of its institutions. The common good is best achieved by a voluntary and personal, interior as well as exterior, commitment of each religious and the common good is the welfare of the whole community and of each one of its parts as a social solidarity.

The responsibility of superiors, as leaders of a community, is to direct the individual religious to achieve the common good, the temporal and eternal salvation of each religious. Their most important function is to adjust the means to the end. The end is not the temporal prosperity of a particular institution, not even the smooth operation and functioning of an establishment, but the growth and development of the individual religious in an atmosphere conducive to a free commitment. This requires constant adjustment and adaptation to the circumstances not always under our control. Our apostolic commitments, teaching, hospital work, social work, are not completely free from outside pressure. They are constantly being influenced by the requirements of a society that is in constant evolution and subject to rapid change. This is modern society, this is a new phenomenon, and religious life will benefit or suffer from this change in proportion as our superiors are alert to the changes and are willing to rethink the religious pattern to fit the demands of modern society.

This effort toward adaptation need not be looked upon as a capitulation to the demands of modern society, thought of as the bad, bad world. It is simply a need to be realistic and alive to the Will of God as expressed in the march of humanity toward a brighter future. It would be unrealistic and also harmful to keep a pattern of rules and regulations reminiscent of the horse-and-buggy stage of human development. God's Will is not merely expressed in the rules and regulations, but also by the march of events and the evolution of society. It is the responsibility of superiors to be sensitive to the new developments and alive to the needs of the religious in terms of adaptations needed to fulfill their commitments to society.

Our Lord Himself counselled His apostles that adaptation was necessary to new circumstances of life. When the Pharisees complained that
the disciples did not fast or observe the purification laws of the Jews,
He forcefully came out in favor of a change. "You cannot put new
wine into old bottles, for the new will burst the old. You cannot put
a new patch on an old garment, or the rip will be greater" (Matt.
9:16-17). Our Lord advised His disciples to forsake the pattern of
obligations imposed by the Pharisaical traditions in favor of a more
realistic religious pattern. Instead of having a set routine of penitential
life, Our Lord promised them the insecurity of a missionary existence with
its share of persecutions, displacements, constant adjustments in shifting
from place to place and from community to community.

The temptation of a religious order is to settle to a comfortable
existence, to equate a smoothly functioning pattern of life with fulfilling
the Will of God in the present order of things. And we know that in
the past religious orders needed reforms and revivals. Not only did
some disappear because their objective ceased to have meaning, the
numerous hospital and military orders of the time of the Crusades, the
redemption of captives, but in order to stay alive, religious orders had
to rediscover their role in the Church and in society. This is a constant
task and it is one highly important task, not merely counselled but commanded by our Holy Father and the Congregation of Religious because
life is not standing still. It is evolving at a rate that is unprecedented.
The problem that confronts every religious community today is a need
to reassess its religious pattern in terms of its commitments to society
in the apostolates for which it is responsible. The primary responsibility
of this assessment belongs to the superiors, although subjects are often
in a better position to suggest revision or adaptation because they are
the ones who most suffer from the tensions created by an outmoded
pattern of religious obligations.

According to the theses of Cardinal Suhard of Paris in his immortal
pastoral letter, *Growth or Decline* (FIDES, 1948), the Church herself
is subject continually to realigning herself with a changing humanity.
There is in her something unchangeable: her origin is divine, her life
is divine, her mission is to lead mankind to God. She is a gift of God
to man and this she cannot change. There is something immutable
about her nature, means and mission. Like Christ, she is divine. Like
Christ she is also human and it is the human aspect of the Church
that is subject to change. To be too identified with any one civilization,
any one culture, or any one period may nullify her mission to all mankind, may isolate her from the very people she has the responsibility to
save. She must be, like her divine Founder, all things to all men and

therefore she must be adaptable to a changing climate, changing habits, changing patterns of human existence.

"To what does the Church owe her successive triumphs?" asks the Cardinal. "To what she knew enough to shed. To grow is to die a little. She knew how to give up in due time and without regret everything that was really only a garb, a temporary fashion, not essential to her mission or her life."

What is true of the Church, is equally true of religious orders. Those that are unwilling to adjust themselves to new conditions of life and of society, that are too attached to outworn formulas, are in danger of mummifying, of petrifying. The appearance is there, but the life is gone out, like the petrified fossils we see in museums.

III. ESSENTIALS OF THE CHRISTIAN LIFE

1. It is first of all a life of union with God, a life of charity. Union with God may be defined as the intimate consent, free and loving, to the Father's Will which makes us like to Him, one with Him in this love which carries us to Him. It is the soul of our life and our activity. "Thou shalt love the Lord thy God with thy whole heart, mind, soul, will and strength" (Luke 10:25). "It is not he who says, Lord, Lord who enters into the Kingdom, but he who does the will of my Father." "I am come to do the will of Him that sent Me." For the Christian it is not otherwise. Fulfillment of God's Will which is indicated to me by the rules and constitutions as approved and by the commands of my superiors. But it is the responsibility of superiors to analyze what the Will of God is in the case of religious and this grave responsibility needs *natural and supernatural prudence*. What does this love of God mean in terms of our profession, professional know-how, professional competence, etc.?

2. The law of the Cross and purification is a fundamental law of the Christian life. "It behooved Christ to suffer and to die and so to enter into the kingdom of heaven" (Luke 24:26). There is always the tension between the two poles of Christian asceticism: on the one hand nature and creation come from the hand of God — they are good, they are for the use of man and for his perfection; on the other hand man needs to learn to use them with detachment and "as if not using them." This is not his final resting place; he is made for higher things, so he must not get wrapped up in them, get lost in them as if they were sufficient for him. This presents the problem of the Cross. "Instead of joy having been set before him, Jesus chose the cross" (Heb. 12:2). Through the passion and death Christ has buried man-

kind's sins so that man can again live in the life of God. But it takes dying, detachment to live the life of a son of God. Through being buried with Christ we have the marks of the crucified in our souls. We must henceforth live a life of union with God.

3. The Religious adds the obligation of the Evangelical Counsels of poverty, chastity and obedience to the obligations of Christian life. Fundamentally these vows are a consecration that was begun at Baptism when we renounced the devil and his works and displays. We are now using the divinely counselled means to make this consecration doubly meaningful. We are putting ourselves in a state of perfection. Because of our religious consecration we are living out with greater singleness of purpose what the Christian is already committed to, the law of universal love and the law of the Cross.

Asceticism is necessary in the life of the Christian, not because the world God has created is bad, not because God has imposed on the Christian an obligation to repair the damage, but because the Christian is buried with Christ to a life of sin and purely temporal involvement to achieve an eternal destiny. The Christian is waiting for the second coming of Christ and must use the present accordingly not by way of final commitment, but as if not using it because for him eternal values are beyond and above. That does not permit him to despise or look down upon the world, but merely not to fall in love with it to the point of being distracted or deterred from his goal which is *union with God*.

This proper attitude toward asceticism is important if we are going to have the right attitude toward the value of particular rules and particular kinds of penance that the rules impose. In other words, as far as the manner of carrying out our ascetical life is concerned, the manner in which we are detached from the present state of society will vary with the particular ethos and climate of the times. Some ascetical practice which may have been conceived in the Middle Ages may have corresponded to the temper of the times and may be quite out of place today. Or even the kind of penitential life that was suited to the nineteenth century may be out of tune with the present state of spiritual climate. The law of the cross is for the Christian an inescapable reality and the only means to his eternal happiness. No Christian can escape the law and be part of Christ, but there may be greater divergence in the manner in which this asceticism is practiced today than there was in previous centuries.

It is of utmost importance for the proper regulation of your subjects' lives to have the right perspective with respect to the kind of spirituality to be advocated in this day and age. And this does not eliminate the particular genius of the different religious orders to emphasize certain truths that are peculiar to them and to witness for Christ either the spirit of poverty in the case of Franciscans, the spirit of contemplation for the Dominicans, the spirit of the worshiping community in the case of the Benedictines, the spirit of discipline and obedience of the Jesuit, etc. These are all aspects of the total Christ, but even these must be practiced in the light of a society that is not at a standstill. The lord and serf relationship of the feudal age, the authoritarian climate of the post-Reformation days, or the democratic, freedom-loving twentieth century must respect authority — but the manner of showing that respect differs widely. We have to espouse our own twentieth century to be effective members of our times. To carry out an apostolate that fits our times and makes our apostolate genuinely Christian *we must incarnate* the present century. We must learn to shed some of the features of the past ages, in order to fit our own and this is what the Holy Father stresses when he urges superiors to consider these changes. He has given us a magnificent example by changing the discipline of the fast and the liturgical practices of the Church. What a boon these changes have been for the faithful! It was an example of stressing the essential and adapting in non-essentials.

IV. ADAPTATION MUST REFLECT NEW SPIRITUAL TRENDS

A spirituality of the twentieth century will necessarily express some of the dominant features of our age. We live in a streamlined age. The emphasis is certainly not on an ornate, overloaded, highly decorative pattern in art, literature, in building, in design. We are functional, we are supremely practical people. This characteristic will find its counterpart in our approach to religious life. Honesty and simplicity are the tone. To quote a contemporary: "It is the religious question which is asked when the architect, in creating office buildings or churches, removes the trimmings taken over from past styles because they cannot be considered an honest expression of our own period, prefers the seeming poverty of a purpose-determined style to the deceptive richness of imitated styles of the past. He knows that he gives no final answer, but he does give an honest answer."

This attitude is typical of the modern spirit and of this modern trend, which would say that it is more conformed to a moral climate than the rich cover-up of the Baroque period or the imitations of the nineteenth century. There is a directness, simplicity and devotion to detail that is marvelously exemplified in the life of St. Therese of Lisieux. Who would deny that God did not send her to show us the way of spiritual simplicity?

Another characteristic of the modern age is vigor and courage. Who would ever have dreamt of the monumental achievements that have succeeded one another and have far outreached anything even dreamed of in past ages. We span oceans, we control sickness, we are at the very doors of discovering the vast universe of the solar system and the vast universe of the atom. This ideal of courage and new initiatives is noticeable in the many new apostolic achievements that have been set afoot during the last fifty years. Our hospitals, our universities, grade and high schools, our social services are vast undertakings. They demand courage and initiative on the part of religious. The spirituality that we propose to our religious must not only fit them to carry out these gigantic enterprises, but must help them to sanctify themselves in the process. St. John Bosco was a prime example of the busy head of a religious order with innumerable religious enterprises and yet who at the same time achieved great sanctity without ever losing the human touch. He is just as much known for educating the least among God's children as for initiating magnificent institutions. Mother Cabrini could be cited as a still more familiar example. We must ask ourselves what in our religious formation and our religious pattern is geared to stimulate and strengthen sanctity in the midst of an active life.

A third characteristic of the modern world is a social conscience, a social awareness, charity in its broadest sense. We are one world, and are fast approaching the day when we shall be one world and while we are very close to one another economically, and technically, we are far apart spiritually. Who will unite the world? asks Cardinal Suhard, will it be the gospel of hate or the gospel of love? We know that Christ wants to unite the world and has entrusted that mission to his Church. We must inject love into the present world. It must be a real love, a heroic love. It must be the kind of love that forgets self completely. A Father Charles de Foucauld would exemplify this love. He decided to carry out his apostolate by living the life of the people and wherever his spiritual sons and daughters are going, whether into the slums of Chicago or the Indian villages of Brazil, the shacks of an Algerian suburb, these religious adapt themselves completely to the surroundings. In a sense they lose themselves to the surroundings. In a sense they lose themselves to incarnate Christ in the lives of the people to whom they are sent. This takes detachment, courage of an exceptional kind. How different the honest portrayal of the lives of saints in our day from the miracle-studded accounts contained in the second nocturne of the daily Office! We are not afraid to be honest about our human failings because we know that God is even more glorified through our infirmities than through our achievements. If there was sin or weakness, or simply human failing in the life of a saint, we like to admit it, even to play it up to show God's infinite mercy.

This trend is reflected in the secular literature of Francois Mauriac, in the realism of Steinbeck, Hemingway or Richard Wright, who portray sordid reality, not because it is sordid, but because it is real and should be exposed for what it is. We are no more scandalized, as were our parents, by Leon Bloy who exposed the hypocrisy, the phony Christian who masqueraded Christianity behind a facade of religiosity. Our spiritual life reflects this honesty and uneasiness before complacency. The very fact that you are here proves that you are not satisfied with the status-quo, that you are deeply concerned with the welfare of your religious and that you are willing to ask for help. I think that this attitude is a great step in the right direction.

Finally, our age, which is a democratic age, has a deep respect for the human person. Democracy does not primarily mean universal suffrage or popular elections. Democracy means, first of all, the primacy of the person, the spiritual value residing in the person as a son of God. America is the natural breeding ground for this kind of philosophy of life and we respect the humanity of a workingman as well as that of a president and we are even proud of the fact that a person can and occasionally does go from errand boy to president of the bank. This respect for the individual, no matter who he is, though it obviously needs to be perfected when it touches the underprivileged, nevertheless is natural to America and quite different from the climate of Europe and the Oriental countries. Again, this will have its repercussion in the religious life, in the freedom and initiative that are allowed to the religious in the responsibilities that are confided and undertaken. The Church in this country has certainly benefited by this spirit of enterprise and we are grateful for the unprecedented freedom of action that is allowed to the religious orders in expanding their establishments and developing new enterprises. We must ask ourselves if our religious pattern is conducive to developing human personalities and allowing them full play in the development of their talents and potentialities. To suppress or thwart human initiative and personal endowments would not merely be against the good economy as understood by our age, but would also be against the obvious will of God. God wants to be glorified by His creatures in a fully developed human personality.

Modern asceticism must take into account these wonderful qualities of the present age, if it is to fit the exercise of the apostolate and attain the personal development of human personality. Simplicity and functional effectiveness, vigor and courage, social awareness and a greater appreciation for the human person are great achievements of our age and will leave their mark on our spirituality as climates of the past ages have left their imprint on their respective spiritualities. Tomorrow we shall consider some of these different periods of ascetical history, if only to help us to see what is essential and enduring in asceticism and what is changing and subject to discard in a different context.

Like the life of Our Lord who is the prime example, the lives of saints are filled with these tensions between outlived forms and new needs of society. Saints were generally forward-looking people who tried to be above the pettiness of their day and age. But they were firm in keeping their sights on God and on the divine will expressed through their period of history.

Heroism is called for to make the necessary adjustments and beneficial adaptations.

II

Short Historical Review of Christian Asceticism

The purpose of this morning's conference is to give us a historical glimpse of the different trends of asceticism in the Church. The purpose is specifically to demonstrate that the ascetical practices changed with the times to fit the pattern of an evolving society.

As we pointed out in the first talk, there are certain aspects of the life of the Christian which are of permanent value, which do not change. The first is obviously that charity or union with God is the primary end of all Christian striving. The first commandment is always the first: Love the Lord thy God with thy whole mind, heart, will, soul and strength. This had been first in the Old Testament; our blessed Lord reaffirmed its priority and quickly added the second: Love thy neighbor as thyself. This is the whole law and the prophets.

A second reality that must be kept in mind as vital and essential is the law of the Cross. No other way leads to salvation than through being identified with Christ who saved humanity through the Cross. Because mankind is tainted with original sin, and actual sin, and because there is a lack of balance or integrity which has to be established, the law of penitential purification is part of every Christian's life. No salvation except through the Cross.

What has differed throughout the centuries of Christianity is the manner in which this cross was carried as an expression of genuine love of God and neighbor. This has varied with the different cultural climates, the different needs of society, the different temperaments.

A quick study of these moods or practices may throw a light on the needs of rethinking our penitential or ascetical practices in the light of the needs of contemporary society.

I. Apostolic Times

Already St. Paul had to warn the Colossians against adopting the ritualistic practices of the Jews. "Let no one, then, call you to account for what you eat or drink or in regard to a festival or a new moon or a Sabbath . . . "

St. Paul's major thesis was that the Christians, from Gentile or Jewish origin, were freed from the yoke of the Jewish legal system. They had attained the freedom of the children of God. They were not to be subject to the purifications, the legal observances of the old law which were the shadow of mysterious realities of the new dispensation.

Christ Himself has put a new soul into the law when He interiorized the precepts of the law. "It was told to you of old, Thou shalt not kill. I say, do not hate. . . . Thou shalt not foreswear thyself, but I say, do not swear at all . . . thou shalt love thy neighbor, love thy enemy." He wanted fasting, almsgiving, prayer to be practiced for God with purity of intention.

To the Pharisees, He had some harsh words to say because they possessed the keys to the kingdom, but did not open up the door for others and they themselves did not enter into it. They posed as saints and interpreters of the law, but used it to plunder the widow and the orphan.

But St. Paul in the footsteps of Christ asked his early Christians to endure the Cross of Christ in the guise of persecutions, misunderstandings and innumerable hardship with joy. Not because things in themselves are bad. He maintained that if he did not use marriage like the apostle Peter, it was not because he did not have perfect right to it, but because for the sake of the Gospel celibacy was preferable. He recommended the Cross not merely for the sake of being in trim and detached, like an athlete, the better to run the race and achieve the prize. He practiced heroic abstinence, heroic trials which he recounts in the Second Epistle to the Corinthians, for the sake of Christ and the Gospel, for the sake of the Kingdom of God.

It is interesting to note in the Gospels the frequent question asked by the doctors of the law: Which is the first and greatest commandment? The background of this overriding concern is the fact that the scribes had accumulated 614 precepts to be observed and it was not easy to choose among that number any satisfactory scale of priority. So they came to the conclusion that they were all equally important. What to do when there was conflict? That is the spot where the scribes and doctors of the law were able to twist the knowledge they had to their own advantage.

In the question of meats consecrated to idols, St. Paul feels entirely free to eat the meat; idols are nothing. But if in doing so, this leads a brother into sin, because he has a weak conscience, then it were better not ever to eat meat. "And thus through thy enlightenment, the doubting soul will be lost; thy brother, for whose sake Christ died. When you thus sin against your brethren, by injuring their doubtful consciences, you sin against Christ. Why then, if a mouthful of good is an occasion of sin to my brother, I will abstain from flesh meat perpetually, rather than be the occasion of my brother's sin" (I Cor. 8:13).

II. ASCETICISM IN THE PATRISTIC AGE: MONASTICISM

Christ promised that after His death His disciples would suffer persecution and be dragged before governors and kings, be put to death even by their own countrymen and relatives. They were not to be disappointed. The early ideal of Christian life was virginity and martyrdom. These were not entirely new. The Jews practiced virginity — witness St. John the Baptist and the Essenes. The heroic endurance of the Maccabean martyr was not unnoticed as an ideal. What Christ brought into the picture was that His followers were to strive for this ideal while awaiting the second coming of Christ.

But gradually Christianity got to be accepted, got to be recognized officially and the danger did not now come from the side of a persecuting government but from a watered-down Christianity which did not require any particular heroism or sacrifice. One could fully enjoy this life *and* life everlasting. To avoid this extinguishing of the Christian spirit in materialism, the spirit of Christ called souls into the desert to live a life of heroism and asceticism not known to the pagan world. It was not to flee society that the chosen souls peopled the desert, but to be able to live the Christian life in its purity. And soon, to avoid individualism and the eccentric in this ascetical or eremitical life, these monks grouped themselves into communities. The great ideal of monasticism begins to play a preponderant role for all Christendom. The Benedictine ideal was to live the Christian life in the security and tranquility of the monastic community which worked for its own livelihood, put the *opus Dei,* the work of God, in its proper place and gave hospitality to the needy and the homeless. Each institution had its school; learning and science were preserved and marvelously encouraged so that the monastery became the refuge of nobility and the center of culture during a very turbulent period of Europe's history.

The ideal of the monastic community was not extreme asceticism, but liberation from the world and its concerns whether that be carving out a livelihood or carving out a kingdom. This renunciation must be spiritual as well as material. The emphasis was interior or spiritual renunciation through the practice of physical renunciation. It was abstention from possessing one's own income, abstention from having one's own family, abstention from doing one's own will, in other words, liberation rather than affliction. We know that St. Benedict had a horror of individualistic practices. He wanted to save the itinerant monk from the danger of doing his own will and losing himself. The ideal of the eremitical or solitary life was never forgotten; not only do we have it incorporated in the communities founded by St. Bruno, the Carthusian and the Cistercian, but even St. Benedict had a place for the hermit after the monk had practiced his Christian virtue in the framework of a community. The eremitical ideal still remained the ideal toward which the monk aspired. But it was reserved for the perfect, the monk who had been tried in the practice of virtue in the framework of obedience.

The monastic ideal inspired the whole of the early Middle Ages so much so that even the secular clergy imitated it and we have the beginning of the cathedral chapters, the canons regular and the whole pattern of community living imitating this monastic ideal. We are still greatly influenced by this ideal in our liturgical practices. Communion fast, morning Mass, the Church year are largely monastic practices. The monastic age continued essentially the ideal of the patristic period: abstention from comfort and luxury the better to overcome the temptation of the new Christian society — the attraction to possess this life with no sacrifice. Chastising the body with fasting, flight from comfort, were the principal practices of the monks throughout the western and eastern parts of Christendom. Positively, it represented an orderly fulfillment of prayer, especially as it was enshrined in the seven hours of a day, interspersed with study and work. The monastery was to be self-sufficient and provide for the needs of the traveler and dependent peasant. We must remember that it was a time of constant turbulence and insecurity. Invasions from barbaric nations from the East and the North and later from the Islamic forces to the South were a constant threat. The monastery provided an oasis of peace and tranquility.

III. The Medieval Period: The Mendicant and Itinerant Fraternities

With St. Francis, who was preoccupied with bringing the Christian message into the newly rising urban communities through the example of itinerant bands of brethren who preached the Gospel by example still more than by word, this monastic ideal received a strong flavor of conformation to the crucified Christ. It was the time of the Crusades. The Holy Land was uppermost in the minds of the Christians. St. Francis himself made a journey to the Holy Land which has retained a strong Franciscan tradition. The Franciscan cowl is a familiar sight in Jerusalem and the Christian centers of the Holy Land. The asceticism practiced is generally the same as in the time of the desert Fathers except for the marked emphasis on the poverty of the Christian to imitate the One Who did not have where to lay His head. This Gospel message was designed to offset the richness and luxury of the newly arrived burgher, or bourgeois, the city dweller. The opulent centers of commerce brought about by the increase of commerce between East and West, accumulated immense wealth which most often ended in great rivalries between cities and between famous houses and families. We know that St. Francis was engaged in one of these wars and subsequent incarceration led to his conversion.

Because Christianity was cooped up in great monastic centers, there was widespread religious ignorance among the ordinary people, servants and country folk. To come to the remedy of this, St. Dominic originated his itinerant friars to preach the Gospel to the poor. And we know that the practice of the Rosary became their great instrument of popular devotion. It was bringing the equivalent of the Holy Office to the people.

Conformity with Christ and Christ crucified brought in the practices of scourging, of bearing a crown of thorns, of wearing chains and giving one another discipline. And we notice some extreme cases of this, like Blessed Henry Suso and the Flagellants of St. Vincent Ferrer, but also the discipline of study which largely replaced manual labor became widespread with the rise of European universities. Active life and contemplative life were not considered as distinct states, but the active life was thought to be the vestibule or the novitiate of the contemplative life. It preceded the contemplative life, like philosophy would precede theology, like apprenticeship precedes the mastery of a trade.

We have a marked extension of the monastic spirituality to the laity through the Third Orders. This put great emphasis on the duties of the states of life while at the same time living a life of poverty, chastity and obedience consonant with the different states of life. Even for these Christians the common life is the rule of sanctity. We see such holy people as St. Elizabeth, St. Bridget and many a king, like St. Louis, either withdraw to the monastery or convent in later years, or surround themselves with monks and friars who would lead their life of regular prayer and study either at the palace or on travel. Pilgrimages became a popular form of penance in this period. Note *The Canterbury Tales.*

IV. MODERN ERA: PERSONAL PIETY

A great change in orientation of spirituality came about in the late Middle Ages and the forerunner to the Protestant Revolt. Let us call it the Era of Personal Piety with the *Imitation of Christ* as the classic of this period. It is a time of strife, of plagues, of disintegrating feudalism and rising nationalism. The vernacular literatures begin to take shape as distinct languages. In Italy, Latin becomes Italian under the brilliant pen of Dante; French takes shape, so does Spanish, English under Chaucer and German under the mighty pen of Luther. People seem to be tired of the existing social framework and seek to express themselves in a strong personal way. It is the age of individual exploit and heroism. Oceans are being crossed and continents discovered. Art and song run riot. The whole world is bursting at the seams. The world of religion is also looking for more personal and interior forms of prayer.

The trend is to a psychological approach to prayer life. Introspection becomes an exciting new science under the masterful lead of St. Ignatius Loyola with his retreats and examination of conscience, of St. Francis de Sales with his well laid plans of prayer life and attention to the duties of one's state of life. We have a sharp break away from the traditional monastic manner of ascetical life and prayer life. Private devotions begin to multiply. The official prayer of the Church loses its central position and often becomes assimilated to private prayer. We know that St. Francis de Sales attempted to send his religious, the Visitation nuns, to visit the home and to do apostolic work outside of convents. The Visitation nuns were denied this ideal and remained a cloistered order. But this indicates a change and in order to keep his Charity Sisters close to the people, St. Vincent de Paul decided to have them not form a religious order.

The Spiritual Director becomes important for the guidance of souls. He is a psychologist who puts the individual soul on a path of human rational plans to seek a life of perfection. The individual and perfection-centered piety is the distinctive mark of this period. It is not difficult to outline this type of spiritual orientation because it is largely what we have fallen heir to. Prayer life is a formal meditation with complicated steps setting imagination, intellect, will, emotions in movement alternately. The Mass up to fairly recent times was more an opportunity of adoring the Blessed Presence, a personal prayer and preparation for Holy Communion rather than a sacrifice in union with Christ. The days are broken up regularly with additional personal prayers, oftentimes prolonging the morning prayer session; then particular examen, again divided into five points at noon. This is followed by a private visit to the Blessed Sacrament, spiritual reading, the Rosary and evening prayers. In between, the Holy Office gets said. The little nosegay recommended by St. Francis de Sales became almost more important than the canonical hours. In the evening before going to bed, proximate preparation for meditation to let our subconscious work on the subject for a successful start the next morning. We are all familiar with this pattern.

The characteristic of this spirituality is that life be very regular and almost exclusively occupied with religious duties. At least there is little interruption by telephone bells; one's schedule is minutely planned. The school children under this ideal setup also follow the same routine and walk around in silence, their arms folded, strictly supervised. I am now thinking of the Jesuit college on a European style, or a private convent school. The students lead a semi-religious life and the elite, in the person of the sodalists, actually make the same religious exercises as the religious with emphasis on daily meditation, particular examen, visit to the Blessed Sacrament and Rosary and even recitation of the Little Office.

The interruptions are taken care of by a bevy of house servants. They run the errands, do the housework. They cook and serve the meals; they answer the doorbell and know exactly where the superior is at each minute of the day and when she can be called to the parlor or when not. Of course for the subject visiting time is strictly scheduled for one day a week or even one day of the month.

Confession, spiritual conferences, monition, chapters of accusation, monthly and annual retreats are all exactly foreseen and foreplanned. A person quickly adjusts to this routine and hopes to communicate the impression of religious preciseness and aloofness to the students. In a busy person's life this horarium either becomes impossible and is not lived up to, or else from sheer exhaustion through catching up with it and making up for missed exercises, a person may have to make difficult choices between neglecting a duty of state of life. In nursing (and I know from personal experience in the hospital) around the busy time of the hospital, at meal time, at cleaning-up time, at the time of the medical visit a patient hardly ever sees a religious on duty. Hence the hospital gets to be run fairly regularly by the student nurses who are on the job at these important times of a sick person's day.

There is work that needs long hours of duty such as the classroom situation, the life of studies, the life of a social worker. A fragmentated religious schedule can run roughshod over the requirements. I think it is important to note that this religious routine presupposed a fairly calm existence not only on the part of the religious but of the students and an army of servants to help take care of the workload and the unexpected needs of the religious. Also it supposed pretty much that the life was lived under one roof, in close association. The life of the students was just as regulated as the life of the religious and every minute of their time was spent under supervision and largely in silence. The number of students was generally fairly small and capable of being personally known and easily advised, like members of a family.

Private spiritual exercises are placed on par with the Mass and the Divine Office. The time allotted to each was carefully calculated to fill the day to the minute. Rising was fairly early and curfew correspondingly early. Let me merely remark that we still have the schedule or horarium, but we do not have the servants, nor the quiet and leisure, nor the small family unit. Our religious run million dollar schools, hospitals, institutions. There are besides religious, often many persons employed with professional status, the work force clock in and out on the minute; the network of social calls and interruptions from the outside world, persons who command respect and cannot be kept waiting knocks schedules all to pieces, besides the need of keeping up with the latest happenings, local, national and international, all of which affect our lives and those of our companions vitally.

The question we are asking ourselves this week is to what extent we have to rethink our lives in this day and age in order to make an impact on society through our full-time apostolic commitments and to go to God through our daily call of duty. There are certain situations of this day that have changed radically from past ages which call for adaptation in order to avoid utter frustration. Let us enumerate a few of these.

The first obvious difference between our age and the past is the tremendous technical advance that has been made. We are children of an age of technology and science. This we cannot bypass even if we are trying to live lives cut off from the world. We need to use the gadgets only because they are time saving and there is no place for the horse and buggy except in a museum or in a zoo or a Disney wonderland. The car is here to stay and society is becoming increasingly more mobile. This means more ease in traveling, but the community is also obliged to rethink its position to car travel which in Europe, where the rules may have been made, may be an unthinkable luxury. Is it better to have Sisters who are used to driving cars while they were in high school or in college before answering the call to religious life, or is it better to impose constantly on good neighbors to haul us around? It is something to think about. The car in this country is not a luxury and in many places like the far West and South, it is a sheer necessity. This problem must be brought to the higher superiors with realism and courage. All the modern communities do not have any problem on that score. They, too, take the vow of poverty.

Then there is the new era of vast communication. The newspaper, the radio, TV have shrunk the world to the point where anything happening on the other side of the globe in the tiniest corner of the earth is immediately a world problem. Then, because of these vast media, which throw new worlds open for investigation to the youngest of our children, it is a different child that we are trying to teach than was the case only fifty years ago. The modern child is informed or misinformed, as the case may be, in matters so vast that it is difficult to teach them unless the teacher knows what she is dealing with. While I am surely not in favor of spending hours before the TV set, nevertheless there is an obligation to be informed about the news or else we are left behind and the children will lose confidence in their teacher. It is something to consider. Keeping properly informed can become a splendid asceticism. The whole area of what to read and where to get the right kind of information is a problem that can call forth much self-denial and wise and prudent choices need to be made. In a sense, it is easier just to stay ignorant and out of step, but is that in line with our mission? Or it is easier, too, just to read what one wants to read rather than what one should read or see. Again asceticism.

Another factor that needs to be worried about is the freedom and initiative that our youngsters are used to and are very often encouraged to develop in our schools. If the children only knew the small amount of initiative or the petty supervision that a religious is often subject to it would not only deter religious vocations, but make them suspicious of our state of mental health. Perhaps a whole batch of former practices that were in vogue, such as opening the mail of subjects, the properly authorized use of phones, the permissions needed to enter a home, the prohibition to eat with strangers or even one's relatives, these practices should be rethought in the light of an American setting. They have risen out of European social settings that are completely outdated. Again, we must not throw the whole framework of ascetic practices overboard as often happens, but we must review our rules and regulations in order to facilitate communication rather than hinder it, provided it gives us a better conrol of our apostolic life. The apostolate and its furtherance should be the key to solving that problem prudently.

Poverty is another area that needs to be aligned with present-day reality. In the past the Church has had to revise its position by relaxing on the regime of the solemn vow to that of the simple vow merely because in the present society, the state would not recognize a condition of renouncing the right of property. And, too, we have a situation where our institutions are not merely million dollar operations, but we have to go begging for funds continually. Every community has become a mendicant in a way that St. Francis never dreamt of. What I am thinking of is not so much the vow of poverty itself, but our relationship to those with whom we live and carry out our apostolate. Are we using the same yardstick, namely poorly rewarded labor, with our employees and are we forever calling on the generosity of the parents of our children? Are we making fund-raising the test of our apostolic success and usefulness? Every community has to have an organization for fund-raising if it wishes to be in a position to expand. Our American economic system is largely responsible for that and we are adjusting to it quickly. The question we must ask is, are we compromising our apostolate teaching, hospital care, etc., by orientating it to fund-raising.

These are all the problems that should make a person fearful of undertaking the job of a superior. On the other hand there is a real problem of rethinking our whole religious life in terms of our modern apostolic commitments to see what needs to be done with our pattern of religious obligations. There is a danger that all the religious obligations lose their ascetic value if too many exceptions have to be made — the horarium, for example, is meant to be kept or it is not anything — or else we compromise our apostolate, our mission to the people who will have a hard time to understand our mode of action and unrealistic attitudes occasioned by our rules and regulations which were designed for another age.

We are all aware, of course, that a wild rush for adaptation is not the answer. Our Holy Father warned us against that but he also warned us against adhering to outworn formulas for the sake of holy tradition. There must be a holy desire to take stock of our commitments to society as well as to God, which is often one and the same. Perhaps a spirituality of action would be one of the keys to solving the problem of adaptation. This we shall probe in tomorrow's conference.

III

Toward a Spirituality of Action

Those of us who are engaged in the active apostolate are frequently confronted with a defense of the apostolate as against the priority of personal sanctification. The argument is generally captioned by the well-known phrase "You cannot give what you do not have." Today we want to examine the validity of this position and in the process to find the key to a spirituality of action that may give us a better basis of spiritual growth and synthesis for the active apostolate.

We are of the opinion that there is a prejudice against the active apostolate. It is generally called activism and how often is there a stigma attached to the performance of any apostolic activity. Interior life is opposed to the exterior life as if one necessarily excluded the other. It is true that *action,* contact with creatures, carries the risk of overextending oneself, but this evil is not inevitable nor is it a necessary consequence.

On the contrary, if we examine the lives of a Paul, of Augustine, of Francis of Assisi, of Francis Xavier, of Vincent de Paul, even of a Teresa or John of the Cross, of John Bosco, we not only see lives of great apostolic activity, but people who grew precisely through their apostolate into giants of the Church. More and more in this day and age we must learn to see in our apostolate a rich source of spiritual growth, a primary means of union with God and certainly not just a temptation or trap toward mediocrity or cessation of prayer life.

Even St. Thomas Aquinas maintained that the ideal of Christian life was not the contemplative life alone, or the active life alone, but the union of the two as we see it so remarkably present in Our Lord's public career.

I. THE ROLE OF ACTION IN THE WORK OF REDEMPTION

The formula that is current concerning the relative value of prayer and the apostolate is that prayer being a primary means of union with God, the more there is prayer and therefore the less there is apostolate, the more there is sanctity. It would seem therefore that every contemplative by the very fact of spending time at prayer would be a sure bet for canonization, whereas those engaged in the apostolate are in constant danger of losing their souls. The problem is really badly stated. We are trying to fit a spirituality that is proper to the monk to someone engaged in the apostolate. There must be a spirituality for those engaged in the active apostolate which is quite different from the spirituality that is properly monastic. Most of our religious engaged in the work of teaching, hospital work and administrative duties as well as social work are engaged in the active apostolate and unless we find in this apostolate the source of our spiritual life, we are doomed to a sorry state of frustration.

The principle of the active apostolate is easy to find: the apostolic action, being the exercise of charity, love of neighbor, is in itself sanctifying. Therefore, far from being an obstacle to spiritual growth and union with God, the apostolic action needs nothing else to be holy. Being an act of charity, the apostolic action and the apostolic life is itself the point toward which the whole movement of the spiritual life culminates through the gift of self. The apostolic action provokes prayer and lifts the soul to self immolation. We could almost reverse the famous formula of Dom Chautard: "Interior Life, soul of the apostolate," to "Apostolate, soul of the interior life."

Does not the common position, namely that prayer life, interior life, must precede the active life have angelistic overtones? As if the life of the soul were somewhat on the margin of, or external to the life of action; as if action were merely an unsavory, unholy corollary of our privileged moments of prayer which are often construed to mean spiritual exercises. There is no doubt that the apostolic life continually needs purity of intention, must be orientated to God and for that purpose moments of prayer, meditation and recollection are of great importance. But does not even a life of prayer and contemplation have the same need of constant pruning of self-will and pride with all its retinue of capital sins? The fact is that man is body and soul, a unity of body and soul, and to deny one or the other is always to err when it comes to analysing human action. It is precisely the Cartesian disdain of action that has given rise to activism (or Americanism as the Europeans call it). It is the disdain of the body that inevitably brings about materialism. Our spirituality must give unity to our life. It would be better to speak of a love-action or of an active love to describe the proper spirituality of the apostolate.

II. Union with God Is the Soul of Apostolic Action

There is even a deeper problem to which we must call attention. It may become clearer if we follow up on our comparison between interior life as the soul and exterior action as the body. The soul is not merely made for maintaining the body. Interior life is not merely for the sake of the apostolate. This would be falling back into the heresy of activism. The interior life, like the life of the soul, is orientated to union with God primarily and this has a value in itself independently of whether there is a work to be done or a contact with the world to be made. In this day of religious indifferentism this value must be strongly affirmed. It would amount to saying that the soul is made to unite the body and keep the body alive. This it surely does; the soul quickens the body. But the soul is not made only for that. Souls are not created to animate bodies, but it is rather the living bodies that are multiplied to permit the awakening of the world of souls. The soul is made for animating and maintaining the body in existence but in view of its own unfolding and to become a gift of God in the human community. Thus union with God is the mainstay of human action and must be pursued by a life of prayer as well as by a life of action.

We are therefore not proclaiming the primacy of effective action as the goal of the spiritual life. We are not interested in prayer life merely to make our apostolate a roaring success. We must not be bewitched by the temptation to aim at a merely human amelioration of life. This would amount to becoming a humanitarian, purely and simply. We must use the world, not lose ourselves in it. We must use it in order to surpass it, to lift ourselves beyond it. This, again, does not mean that we can be slipshod about the way we use this world. The act of true love is ever respectful of all God's creatures. Man does not acquire the moral virtues merely and simply to use the world's goods moderately, or rely on the theological virtues to surpass it, but helped by technology man organizes the world and exploits it by his actions in order to purify it and give it back to God as an expression of love.

The whole thesis, interior *versus* exterior life, is badly stated. Prayer *versus* apostolate is not a realistic approach to solving our need for unifying the two. As a matter of fact, St. Thomas maintains that asceticism precedes contemplation and the latter is the normal culmination of the Christian life for everyone. If we conceive of the apostolate as our ascetic life which helps us to attain union with God, instead of conceiving the apostolate merely as opposed to a life of prayer, then we are on the right road. It is not prayer life which is the goal of the Christian life, but rather union with God is the real end of all man's striving and this union with God can be achieved through the proper use of creation as well as through renunciation of the world. The person engaged in the apostolate of teaching and hospital work and social work is in constant contact with God's creation and the prayer life must sustain that effort and purify that effort rather than compete with it.

If we equate interior life with prayer life, then we are thinking in angelistic terms. We are saying that the activity of soul is alone capable of union with God and that the body has no role to play except to distract us and to lead us away from God. The soul and body are not separate creations. Although the soul is needed to animate the body, it is also true that it is through the body that the soul grows in knowledge and wisdom to its final stage of union with God and is able to become a gift to mankind.

Neither apostolic activity nor prayer life is the goal of life for the Christian, but union with God and this goal must be achieved through the exercise of the duties of our state in life which is the concrete expression of the will of God in our present life. In other words, our life must be so ordered as to achieve in everything we do the glorification of God, "whether we eat, or drink, or whatever else we do." When we do what God wants us to do and when we do this with purity of intention and willingness to forget ourselves and our personal interests then we are truly loving God and neighbor. While this is normally expressed in our rules and constitutions, it is precisely here that the grave responsibility of the superiors and those in charge of our religious institutions lies, to determine with the aid of the Holy Spirit how the modern requirements of our respective apostolates will really and truly unite prayer life and apostolic life to achieve the goal of life in the best way possible, namely union with God.

III. SUPERNATURAL PRUDENCE IS NECESSARY

This requires supernatural prudence. The saints were always on guard against the invasion of personal motives and the propensities of our sinful nature. The reason is simple enough. The apostolate brings us in touch with creatures. While this is not an evil, far from it since creation is given to us to raise us to God (read St. Paul in this connection), this contact is always a risk. Every creature is for us either a springboard to union with God, or a trap limiting our freedom. The sinful tendencies and habits multiply the danger of undue attachment, and therefore increase the risk. To maintain that simply because we are engaged in an apostolic action, everything is pure and holy would be going against all the advice we have from the saints who were ever on the alert for the least movements of sinful nature spoiling apostolic action. St. Leo warns us in one of his Lenten sermons: "That care must be had while engaging in the different pursuits not to soil the religious hearts with worldly dust." He did not say that we had to forego the apostolate.

Do we, therefore, have to maintain an attitude of mistrust toward apostolic activity? How can we give ourselves, heart, mind and soul to our apostolic action (teaching, hospital or administrative work) and still keep that watchful attitude? It is at once a theoretical and a practical problem about which no apostle can be slipshod or indifferent. Here a comparison is very useful. Let us compare interior life to the soul and exterior activity to the body of the apostolically dedicated life. The soul grows and develops through involving itself through the body in the multiplicity of matter, not to get lost in it, but to surpass it, to achieve dominion over it and ascent to God through it. Charity develops through involvement in the world for the sake of going beyond it. "You are in the world but not of the world."

IV. ACTION PROVIDES A STRUCTURE, A BODY TO LOVE OF GOD

Christian charity is not just pious thoughts, or harmless sentiment. It is love in action. Christ Himself expressed it better: "It is not those who plead 'Lord, Lord' who will enter the kingdom of heaven but those who do the will of my Father who is in heaven" (Matt. 7:21). And again, it is the one who says no, but comes through and not the one who says yes and does not follow up who does the will of God (see Matt. 21:28). This is the realism of the Gospel. To think of a spirituality that would consist exclusively of meditations, affective prayer and examination of conscience is not realistic. This would destroy true spirituality as truly as to be engaged exclusively in external activity.

Interior life and exterior activity are not two opposing movements. Both are the expression of God's will. It is in the competent performance of duties of our state in life, as teachers or nurses or administrators that we love God and are committed to the service of our neighbor at the same time. The soul needs its body to arrive at knowledge and self-expression, so our spiritual life needs the works of the apostolate to grow and express its love for God. Is not this the reason why Christ joined the love of neighbor so closely to the commandment to love God, because for all practical purposes it is only through love of neighbor that we have an immediate and tangible way of expressing our love of God. St. John says this significantly in his first epistle: "He who says that he loves God and hates his neighbor is a liar, because how can he love God whom he does not see, when he does not love the neighbor whom he does see."

The soul not only needs the body to formulate ideas and in a sense spiritualize itself by formulating concepts which are spiritual realities, but it also needs the body to express itself, to put over the ideas conceived. In a similar manner charity, love of God and neighbor, needs action to express itself and also to fulfill itself. How can a person love if he does not express the love in some tangible way since love is supremely communicable. To love means to give oneself, soul and body, breath and life. We are to love God with our soul and mind and heart and strength; all of man is involved. To love God is to love the world of human beings for whom He took the trouble to become man and to die for them. To love is to wish another good and to show the sincerity of the love, action is called for.

It is in this perspective that we see the apostles launch into the most daring undertakings, travels into unknown lands, into the very mouth of persecution: St. Paul's adventures; St. Francis goes to see Suleiman the Turk personally; St. Boniface penetrates the deep forests of German barbarism, not to speak of St. Francis Xavier and all the missionaries since his day who braved a world of ignorance, of depravity and religious voodooism. Everywhere there is an opportunity to give God to the world, and to give a part of the world to God. Dissipating ignorance, relieving human ills, sustaining man's courage in the face of insurmountable difficulties, being carriers of peace and salvation. All this is not purely spiritual; the whole human personality, soul and body, is involved just as on the receiving end, the whole man needs apostolic attention. Charity manifests itself and grows through servicing the whole man. Christ came to the rescue of physical ills as much as he cured the spiritual collapse. The apostolate is an act of love no matter at what level it is exercised, in behalf of the witness, or the physically handicapped, as well as in the centers of research or in the heart of universities.

Again this love does not measure itself by the enormity of the undertaking; it can be red-hot in the tiniest acts performed, as St. Therese of Lisieux has shown so magnificently through her way of love. She excelled in the perfection of little things. But even her actions were done through the body and through acts of neighborly service. For man love will always express itself through gift giving, through signs that demonstrate love. Who am I to speak the language of love, sign language, to women whom God has endowed with the secrets of this language. Woman is God's sign language par excellence. She expresses God's maternal love.

V.   ROLE OF SPIRITUAL EXERCISES

Do we forget the need of detachment needed in the apostolate? There is a mystery in the apostolate. It is precisely the balance that is needed between involvement and detachment. A mother must love her child and yet not love it for herself or the love is immediately detrimental to the child. True love is always detached in the sense that it is love for the sake of the object loved and ultimately for the Creator of the object, God Himself. In our apostolate, in our commitments we seek to find the will of God. Christ, I am sure, would have loved to precede Paul into Antioch, Corinth, Ephesus, Athens and Rome, but the Will of the Father was that He go to the lost sheep of Israel and leave the pagan apostolate to His disciples. Such was the Will of the Father. The task of the apostle is to verify, to ascertain at every step: Am I doing the Will of God? What is the Will of God in my life? And if that is important for the religious subject, how much more is it the constant concern of those who represent the Will of God in the person of the superior.

Here we can situate the spiritual exercises. These are a suspension of the apostolate to determine whether we are doing the Will of God. This is their function, therefore in a sense they should be utterly orientated to bolster the apostolate, not so much to assure efficacious apostolate, in the sense of external success, as it should constantly keep the apostle motivated toward doing the Will of God. Even the prompt cessation of external activity when the Will of God calls us to review our actions, is already a sign of wanting to do the Will of God. It demonstrates that we have faith in the grace of Christ which is the real secret of apostolic success. Even here in the performance of the spiritual exercises there is the element of action, in that it is a sacrifice of time that could be allotted to the apostolate. This sacrifice of time, this detachment from activity, this giving up of self in the pursuit of our normal pace of activity, is a sign of doing God's Will, is an act of love of God. It is not that the exercises of piety alone maintain and create the current of love between God and the apostle, it is precisely an act of sacrifice to redirect our own action in the direction of God's Will. According to St. Therese of Lisieux, it was not during her moments of prayer that she had the greatest insights into her mission; it was generally while she was performing very menial tasks, sweeping the corridors, washing the linens, serving the grumpy Sister Peter.

And the apostolate also purifies prayer life. A person could get very attached to the quiet routine of prayer life and not go out of the way to think of anyone else but oneself. The normal routine of a convent or monastery could cloak the greatest selfishness. Not only can the apostolate become a supreme incentive to prayer, ardent prayer and sustained prayer, but sometimes it happens that service of neighbor will disturb the tranquility of our prayer life and also the normal pace of our religious obligations. When it is the Will of God that we come to the rescue of unexpected callers, unscheduled interruptions, even importunate phone calls, prayer life plays the proper role in our life. We must learn to strike a balance, a deep peace of soul in the midst of activity, and that comes from the conviction, sustained by superiors, by directors, and our fellow religious, that we are doing the Will of God.

It is interesting to watch the gradual unfolding of the early Church, how God did not speak directly to Peter and the apostles, but spoke to them through the intervention of events. When the apostles were spending all their time administering to the physical needs of the faithful and perforce they were bound to neglect some members of the growing community, they decided to ordain deacons to serve at table. They unconsciously perhaps were developing the structure of the Church under the pressure of circumstances, true, but also under the influence of the Holy Spirit. When the Church began to settle comfortably in Jerusalem, the Lord stirred up persecution and forced the apostles to flee and carry the Gospel to the ends of the earth. In order to wean the new Christians away from the Jewish ritual and temple worship, the crisis between the Jewish converts and the pagan converts was solved in favor of the pagan converts. All through history, it has been the march of events that has been the finger of God guiding the destiny of mankind and of His Church. It takes prayer and reflection, however, to discover the Will of God in these events and the same is true in one's personal life and the apostolate that is entrusted to us through the voice of superiors.

In order to achieve complete purification in one's apostolate, it is not enough to try to achieve purity of intention; God will put his mark on it by means of passive purifications. It is the trials and disappointments and sometimes the collapse of one's apostolate or apostolic undertakings that speak of God's Will to us in terms that make us really bleed. Again it is an act of faith and a loving attachment to the Will of God that will alone help us in those moments of severe trial. God's Will be done.

VI. Union with God Draws Out Apostolic Action and Sustains It

The soul is the terminus of the activities of the body. The soul quickens the body and organizes its actions so that all the riches of knowledge and love are brought to the fore. The same union with God is the great lever of apostolic action and makes it flower, makes it expand and grow.

Union with God originates apostolic action for it is the Will of the Father that every creature manifest the Glory of God, that every voice sing His praises in the awareness of Christ and in union with Him. St. Paul has a magnificent passage in this respect: "You, however, are not carnal but spiritual, if indeed the Spirit of God dwells in you. But if anyone does not have the Spirit of Christ, he does not belong to Christ. But if Christ is in you, the body, it is true, is dead by reason of sin, but the spirit is life by reason of justification. But if the Spirit of Him Who raised Jesus from the dead dwells in you, then He Who raised Jesus Christ from the dead will also bring to life your mortal bodies because of His Spirit Who dwells in you" (Rom. 8:9-11).

Union with God sustains apostolic action. Love seeks union. Love finds union precisely in doing the will of the beloved, the Will of God. All actions, done for that purpose, become an occasion for progress and growth: "My food is to do the Will of my Father." Apostolic action will be for the one who seeks the Will of God in his life like the food that is assimilated and transformed into one's system. Instead of being an obstacle to virtue, or an obstacle to spiritual growth, apostolic action becomes the very food that creates a greater strength and a greater zest for manifesting the love for God and the glory of God. It is the loving union to the Will of God that produces the hunger for apostolic action and an apostolic life.

Finally, union with God gives effectiveness to apostolic action. Just as the soul empowers the body to act on and to dominate the material world, so it is through love or charity that the apostolic action becomes supernaturally effective. This supernatural effectiveness depends entirely on the degree in which the apostolic action is inserted into the divine economy of redemption. Redemption is not merely something to do, however necessary and important the work might be, running a hospital, organizing a school, etc., but it is a *grace* to be obtained through union with Christ. Redemption is the apostolate, but it is also and above all a grace. The work of redemption requires human involvement, but it is first of all a grace to be obtained for those whom our apostolate benefits.

How do we obtain this grace? Through matching generosity with generosity, love with love. The gift of God asks for the free gift of the apostle himself. There is an exchange of wills. This is the act of love. God gives Himself first and that gift asks for a free commitment of the apostle. We have only to give ourselves totally to God in doing His Will in the state of life that we have placed ourselves, or that God has placed us in. And the summit of this disposal of self into the hands of God is the Passion. It is the supreme sign that God has accepted our total gift and that He is in complete control of all the movements of our nature. And this passion united to the Passion of Christ at Mass becomes the center of our life and of all our striving. There we offer everything, our life and our death, already accepted and incorporated into Christ's supreme sacrifice.

It is this union with God, this desire to do the Will of God in all things that impels the apostolic action and sustains it. It is this union with God which gives it its supernatural effectiveness and culminates in the hour of passion. It is the soul of the apostolate. The apostolate is the expression of God's Will in our life. What we need is to keep it purified and united to the Will of God. Again, this is best accomplished through the apostolate rather than apart from it or prior to it. The acts of prayer and religious exercises are a suspension of the apostolate to keep it in the right direction. They should therefore be for us keyed toward the apostolate and not to thwart it.

The important conclusion that we must draw from this conference is that it is the responsibility of the superiors to analyze the total apostolate of their community, to see how this apostolate is situated into the total mission of the Church and then to adapt the horarium, the routine of the community to this apostolate. It is not the other way around. In the active apostolate it is the apostolate which should be the barometer that will determine the life of the community and the religious exercises must be a real aid, not a hindrance to the performance of the apostolate. It is this that the Holy Father has in mind when he called all religious orders to the challenge of rethinking their constitutions and putting them in line with the requirements of present-day life.

IV

Social Dimensions of Asceticism

We have tried to establish in our first conference what the final goal is of all asceticism, namely union with God, and this union can be achieved through the apostolate or service of our neighbor. The apostolate should be one of the best means of love of God. Christ showed us the way by His teaching and example.

In the second conference we reviewed the principal periods of ascetical practice in the Church in a very quick glance just to show us that asceticism does have a dynamism, a vitality that it borrows largely from the social climate surrounding the Christians of any one period and the need to demonstrate the true Christian spirit in reaction to the principal obstacle to the Christian life of any one period. Example: the ascetic practice of itinerant poverty of the early Franciscans in the face of a new rich, pleasure-minded urban society.

In the third conference we tried to formulate the need for an asceticism of action with the apostolate as the chief characteristic of the modern world. Society is in the process of becoming highly organized, highly professional. To keep any effective contact with the world we must be involved, committed. We cannot be removed from the world and at the same time run institutions that are very much part of the world. Hence the need of a spirituality that will draw maximum effort of dedication and consecration to one's duties of state in life and back up this effort by an appropriate spirituality.

In this fourth conference we are asking ourselves what social dimension does enter into this kind of spirituality. For asceticism to be interiorly effective it must be personal and on the other hand the social climate also exercises a strong influence. What is this influence that could easily make asceticism formalistic and empty of meaning? What are some other conditions that will revive asceticism to keep in touch with the present needs of society?

The final conference will preoccupy us with the basic principle of all asceticisms, how to be a son or daughter of the Church.

Depth psychology and sociology are opening new worlds of knowledge with respect to the behavior of people and the influences that motivate and orientate the activity of souls. Psychology and psychiatry are beginning to discover the world of the subconscious that was not at all known to our founders and their successors. What used to be considered chronic disobedience in the case of a religious may be due to some insecurity or failure on the part of a father or mother in the early stages of upbringing. What looks like an overweening self-asserting character may be the result of a cover-up of an inferiority complex.

In a similar manner, society has a way of exerting pressures that make a person do things that normally would not be done, or would be considered infantile. There is no doubt that in the fervor of a nascent community under the powerful influence of a founder, the weekly accusation of faults must have had its ascetical value. This depends on a frank, sincere, completely honest avowal of one's shortcomings. It is meant not merely as an act of humiliation on the part of a religious, but an act of community by which not merely the good things are shared, but even one's shortcomings. It was an act of laying oneself open to all; for all to see us as we are. Does this condition prevail in the week-to-week Chapter of Accusation? I still have to see this practice have medicinal values either for the individual or the community. The practice of public flagellation which was very commonly used in the latter days of the Middle Ages and practiced by the Friars Preachers had something of the infantile in it, even something of the morbid, which would not be very acceptable in today's society. We live in a different climate, a climate that is sensitive to the deeper motivation of such acts of public penance, a climate that does not understand the physical punishment as a means of witnessing for God. Simon Stylites has his modern counterpart in the marathon tree and flagpole sitters but who would undertake the same kind of eccentric penance in this day or age for the sake of the kingdom of God? We would not hesitate to suspect such a one's motives. Society would be quick to accuse him of seeking publicity and notoriety and the hierarchy would be quick to stop the nonsense.

We know, for example, that society, sometimes even Catholic parents, has difficulty reconciling the call of God to the religious life with rational behavior. We are a sign of contradiction and a reminder that there are realities beyond the temporal realities. But if they see us react to their puzzled concern by a total devotion to our job of teaching or of caring for the sick, if they see in the religious wholesome, integrated personalities, they will be led to detect in us a reality that transcends the natural and can but lead them to God.

I. WHAT DETERMINES THE ASCETIC VALUE OF PENITENTIAL ACTS?

There is nothing more personal than asceticism. Its function is to render the soul more accessible to God, to purify the soul in its ascent to union with God. God has the initiative in loving us, His creatures, but in us charity meets with obstacles, selfish and unredeemed areas that need to be cleared. In each of us there are hills to be leveled and valleys to be filled before Christ can make His triumphal entry. Asceticism, therefore, is a normal and necessary result of a charity in an imperfect and partially bad nature. At the same time, it is a condition and a means of progress in charity. In fact, the source of an increase in grace lies essentially in fidelity to grace already received. And asceticism is nothing else than the extension in all of our nature of the movement of charity in such a way as to make of us an instrument for its action. Faithfulness in asceticism attracts an increase of charity. We thus see the exact place of asceticism in the Christian life.

We are living in a society that has swung from the extreme of a Puritanical-Jansenistic attitude to a completely opposite natural one. Each has a definite attitude toward asceticism. For the Puritan (and our institutions still have puritanical traditions) sex, for example, is a manifestation of man's sinful nature. Man's ideal is freedom from sex and if this is impossible because of concupisence, sex must be severely treated and controlled. Self-control is nigh impossible, therefore industry, sobriety, vigilance are to be encouraged to counteract man's natural depravity. With self-discipline being nigh impossible, modesty and chastity must be achieved through external discipline, supervision and repressive means. A regime of fear is the only deterrent. Strict discipline, external safeguards are multiplied. There is a deep mistrust of human nature.

The free-love ethics of our day has swung to a completely opposite position. Sex, for example, is a biological fact and therefore out of control of the rational faculties. The greater the freedom of sex expression the better society will be and it should guarantee this freedom by appropriate legislation. The results of the practice of chastity and modesty in an attempt to stifle the sex urge is a futile undertaking since in any event the sex instinct obtains satisfaction. At the same time it is unhealthful to repress it because that leads to neuroses and unnatural sex practices. Any kind of singularity in unmarried persons is immediately suspected as a neurotic condition. The Kinsey Report makes homosexuals of all of us; homosexual, heterosexual are his only two classifications.

The Catholic view is just in the middle. Sex is part of a larger pattern. It has a very important social function, the upkeep of the race and the spiritual as well as physical development of the individual. The virtue of chastity regulates the exercise of sex to make it produce maximum results in terms of fruitful love and personality development. Chastity and modesty are virtues to be acquired and while difficult they are by no means impossible. Grace is there to help in the effort to conquer concupiscence. Instead of being harmful, it is very conducive to health and rational existence.

Our forefathers, under the influence of the Jansenist-Puritanical ethics, had a profound distrust of human nature and believed in severe external discipline in order to keep the helpless human nature in check. Our rules and regulations sometimes reflect this kind of social philosophy.

The modern, freedom-loving attitude has a completely optimistic and unbridled confidence in human nature and therefore will be restless at restraints and attempts at discipline. The prevalence of juvenile delinquency is certainly a fruit of this kind of attitude and there is plenty of delinquency on a minor scale that is not even recorded in the papers.

The answer to the modern problem is *self-discipline*. And this must be not only our aim in educating our children or in guiding our youth, but it is also the best solution to the development of human personalities among our religious. There are several ways of achieving regular discipline. One of these is community asceticism.

II. SIMPLE IMITATION OR FOLLOW-THE-LEADER PRINCIPLE

The freer the commitment of the members, the more intelligent the guidance they get from their superiors, the better, too, will be the end product in terms of mature personalities and apostolic effectiveness. Hero worship, exhibitionism are justifiable and effective means of a moral nature. However, personal magnetism and especially the hard authoritarian hand may keep human personalities from developing. Good leadership is the kind that knows how to apportion responsibility and to allow others as much elbow room as possible consonant with the common good. This problem has been brought up during other sessions of this week, so that I need not tarry longer on the problem. It is, however, a central problem for authority, this development of human personality among the religious. Maturity grows with responsibility and freedom of action and a climate that permits the exercise of initiative.

III. REGULAR DISCIPLINE AS A RESULT OF GENERAL LAW

Regular discipline may or may not have an ascetic value depending on whether it is practiced with charity or merely out of a desire for conformity, for the sake of not being out of line with the superior's good pleasure, or community routine. Community life is essentially asceticism practiced in common. Eating in common, seeking permissions for daily needs, silence, the religious habit, all these penitential practices can be done instinctively or by purposeful reflection. I can tell myself that others have done it before me, that I am a member of the community, I follow their example; it is easy to do, the line of least resistance. Does this attitude, which may result in a well-run house, permit a real spiritual development or indicate religious fervor? Is it conducive to a growth in sanctity or personal consecration? Does this kind of automatic living out of the rule make for a successful religious community life?

Law, custom or institution can make of a set of rules mere routine and lose all personality and ascetic value. This is a universal fact. Revolutionary movements are always very loud in clamoring for free expression while they are without responsibility, but once in the saddle, they become opposed to all change and realignment. This is a sociological fact. The same can happen in a community. Occasional change, a break in the routine is advisable even if it is merely reversing the roles as when the youngest religious runs the superior's office on Holy Innocents day, as it happens in some communities. It is in this same spirit that the new legislation is asking for a periodic change of superiors, and also that superiors drop back into the ranks. An exaggerated rigidity is not a healthy situation for the development of human personalities and the flowering of personal consecration to an ideal. Routine generates conformity and comfortable stagnation. Again, the apostolate can serve a good turn by keeping superiors and religious discipline constantly on the alert because it obliges one to weigh the value of the good of souls against the good of a regular life. Constant problems are raised. On-the-spot decisions have to be made, adjustments to new situations have to be considered. Inflexibility in the law or rules leads to formalism and legalism. This in turn breeds phariseeism. A religious person can observe, for example, an exemplary and meticulous material poverty and yet not suffer any of the hardships and hazards of modern economic society. The apostolate will keep us close to people to whom we are sent and will keep us in communion with the social realities and help us to evaluate our personal commitment and responsibility to God and to society.

Another result of a frozen set of observances is the attachment to detail. The law of the spirit, the great laws of life, natural morality or Christian mysticism get no place; they remain unreal and distant in a community that is completely isolated from the apostolate, completely ruled by law or custom. Details or minutiae, on the contrary, become ritual, furnishing the texture of life in common, becoming the arbiter, umpire of the law, reassuring consciences including the conscience of the superior, who satisfies her sense of duty by reminding subjects of the laws and adding her own decrees. In this situation, anyone who has a mind of her own is a disturber of the peace. Is it a sin to have a mind of one's own? Did not God give each one of us a mind to use and to think with? Through the apostolate we can bring freshness and spirit into the law, because the law will always yield to the spirit, if it is enlivened by the spirit of love.

IV. COMMUNITY MYSTIQUE

The law of the spirit — it is the law of mystical solidarity, planted within each community. Mystique can be defined as a heroic faith. It is created by a concurrence of minds and wills forming a kind of communitarian mystique. This often expresses the most profound instincts of the Christian Gospel. The primitive Church gives a good example of this. The pooling of resources and weaknesses among the early groups and fraternities is true of all foundations or religious orders. The problem is how to re-enkindle this kind of fervor, this kind of mystical union which existed at the beginning of a religious community or under certain dynamic reformers. We can do this again through the apostolate. In working with others in the apostolate, whether of teaching or nursing or at the beginning of all kinds of new institutions we can again revive the fervor of the community. We are able to touch again with the finger this phenomenon where all are united, all expressing themselves fully for the common goal. United to Christ, this is nothing other than the Mystical Body of Christ.

I have experienced this real community in groups of lay apostles who made me want to get a similar experience of community among our own religious. It is an experience that makes one hanker after this communitarian ideal where there is a real sharing of ideas and talents, where there is a real communication between different people who all make their ideas known, not for the personal benefit they can get from it, but for the good of the community. Of course, every person benefits by this because they are challenged to the maximum of their powers and talents. There is a beautiful balance that puts at the disposal of one's fellow man the resources that one disposes of and that does not disturb the union established between God and the soul. This community ideal is precisely the Christian alternative to both extremes of today's philosophies, the individualism of capitalist society, with its everybody-for-himself motto, and the communist society, everybody for the collectivity. Here everybody is most benefited by the challenge he received from association and the community is a communion of persons. This is what the little groups of the apostolic college must have been under the dynamic leadership of Our Lord. It carried over into later life when Our Lord has ascended to His Father.

It is difficult to revive this kind of mystique in the general community pattern, but it is possible to have it present among people who have the same professional task to perform. There is no reason why teachers of religion in a school, or teachers of music, or teachers of English or math, if the school is big enough to have several people teach the same subject, could not get together to work toward the formation of a common philosophy of their subject, or find out how to improve their teaching, or lighten one another's task through mutual assistance, keeping one and all informed on the requirements of the field of competence. So much more can be done by a group through team work than alone by oneself. We can touch there this community mystique that makes a person transcend himself and find in his fellow religious a real brother, a real guide to greater life and health and love. Community must be experienced and it can be done only if we are pooling our resources willingly and generously with people of common interests and ideals.

Is this forming a clique? No, provided the group is open to the rest of the community and willing to share its spirit and resources with the rest of the community. This idea that any time two or three religious get together it is for the purpose of plotting against the superior or becomes a threat to the rest of the community, is infantile, an immature attitude on the part of authority or religious. It is something left over from the puritanical church we talked of earlier. On the contrary, this should be encouraged, I think, and our religious need this team work for their own healthy mental development and also as an experience of community which is often very difficult to achieve in the large numbers that constitute our present communities.

God has made man social. This is a need for man. It is through the family, through the intermediate associations, such as the school, the corporation, the union that he achieves goals that he cannot achieve by himself and he receives still greater benefits through being a member of a nation, of the world community, and finally of the Mystical Body of Christ. These different degrees of community living all are designed to perfect the individual and the individual achieves maturity by making his contribution to all these societies of which he is a member. But more than that, he needs his fellow man in order to know himself by a lively exchange of ideas and ideals. A community where communication is not encouraged is really offending against the very creation of God. There is a reason for silence and recollection, but there is equally a time for communication and both need to be encouraged. If this communication is encouraged merely on a light vein, merely at times of recreation, then we may stay condemned to immaturity. As professional people we must encourage this current of ideas especially on a professional level. Both kinds are needed for ourselves, so that we can grow in our competence (and please this should not be construed as bragging or vanity) or else we can never communicate on a professional level when we are thrown in with professional people, clergy or religious of other communities, or even professional people among non-Catholic groups. This lack of communication on our part is a shocking thing to outsiders. This is not witnessing for God, but shirking a responsibility.

A large community is difficult to realize unless we have experience of community on a small basis. This is an education in itself and it is a great help for good human living and the practice of charity.

A current of charity is the best climate in a community. But charity is essentially communicative. We communicate not only patience and humility, but we must also communicate ideas and concerns, and enthusiasm and love for work and interest in other people. Charity means all this and it is best experienced in small groups with common interests. Our rules are entirely too much preoccupied with eliminating cabals and cliques. If we were taught and encouraged more to work in teams on our professional responsibilities, charity would get a tremendous field for operation and it would lighten the burden of individuals, as well as of superiors. In our individualistic society we must learn community. Not the community forged by a Hitler or a Stalin, not the community established by routine and custom, but a community formed by real people who vibrate with the same love for their job, and for their companions of work, and for the people they work for, and for all the people whom their common interests bring together. This is real community and this is the foundation of the Mystical Body. This kind of community informed by grace is the Mystical Body of Christ.

"Wherever two or three are gathered together in My Name, I am in the midst of them." Christ did not restrict this to times of prayer, but to all situations in which obedience brings us together.

V

Living the Rhythm of the Church

The best way to accomplish our task of adaptation in ascetical matters is to live in the spirit of the Church. After all, every religious community is a partial segment of the greater community, the Mystical Body of Christ. They all have different functions, and different ideals and yet they make a beautiful pattern when they realize their unity in the Mystical Body. St. Paul's famous 12th Chapter to the Corinthians applies to us.

> There are different kinds of gifts, though it is the same Spirit who gives them, just as there are different kinds of service, though it is the same Lord we serve, and different manifestations of power, though it is the same God who manifests His power everywhere in all of us. The revelation of the Spirit is imparted to each, to make the best advantage of it. . . . But all this is the work of one and the same Spirit, who distributes His gifts as He will to each severally (I Cor. 12:4-11).

Because we are children of secularistic mentality, which consists in separating religion and life, we have a difficult time to conceive of our functions as teachers, as nurses or administrators, as not having any place in the divine concept of things. As a matter of fact, it is when we do these things in a big way as we do them today that we are the Church teaching, Christ teaching, the Church healing, Christ healing, the Church governing, Christ governing, the Church sanctifying, Christ sanctifying. Just as in the family circle when the father and mother conceive and rear their children, it is the Church that is conceiving and rearing them.

Living with the Church does not merely mean living out the liturgical calendar, or participating with the Church in the mysteries of Christ on the altar. It means still more: for us it means being the Church in our mission to society. The mysteries of the Church will go on without us, but the Church will not be acting in the world, that portion of the world to which obedience assigns us unless we carry out our apostolate. In a sense, we are indispensable to the Church. And it is precisely this contribution that we have to make to society in our professional capacity, which must witness for the Church and for Christ.

Being a witness to Christ in the context of our present society means also being in communion with the other members of the Church and being conscious of the whole mission field of the Church. This is possible for the first time in the history of the Church since the new world has shrunk to the point of being capable of being viewed in one glance. On the other hand, life has become so complicated that we can be really competent only in a small sector of it. Both conditions require that we be in communion with all the members and at the same time responsible for our sector of responsibility.

I. A TREMENDOUS MISSIONARY CURRENT IS COURSING THROUGH THE RANKS OF THE FAITHFUL

So many things have happened to the whole of the apostolate in the last fifty years since the pontificate of St. Pius X, that the Church hardly resembles itself a century ago. The development of the place of the laity in the Church, the secular institutes with their emphasis on nearness to the scene of activity, the liturgical revivals, the Biblical renewal, not to speak of the many changes that are taking place from day to day in the growth of religious communities and their ever-expanding institutions. In the words of our Holy Father the Church is experiencing another of its springtime renewals. This is indeed consoling, but we must participate in this spirit of rhythm to be fully a member of the Church.

The lay apostolate alone has achieved a great impetus through the encouragement of the great popes we have had, but also through the growing in awareness of their membership in the Church. This is not something to be jealous about; on the contrary, the Holy Father has pleaded especially with the religious communities to lend their help both in offering personnel and in generously loaning their physical plants to their sessions and meetings and conventions, which serve for the formation of the lay apostle. We must be aware of the grassroots growth of these apostolates in order to encourage them, especially in our training centers, educational institutions and schools of nursing. At the present the Catholic Action movement is still largely a youth apostolate and therefore still very much under our guidance. There must be among us understanding and spirit of cooperation. This may look like real asceticism, a lot of giving on our part without apparent receiving since we are striving to educate these youths to be leaders in the layman's world, but it will benefit the communities, too, not only in terms of some very apostolic vocations, but also because these lay groups bring us and keep us in touch with the problems of the world without our having to get too immersed in them. They can be marvelous go-betweens of the community and the world. The apostolic lay person is in contact both with institutional Catholicism and the secular world.

The secular institutes can perform the same function especially in a professional capacity. Their freedom from institutional living provides an excellent opportunity for them to mingle more freely in circles of the political, the professional or the economic world. They can help us be in touch with the thought and orientation of the professional world. Again, instead of looking upon them as competitors, we can welcome their help and their specific contribution to the Mystical Body of Christ. On the other hand we can again help them by providing them with the guidance and retreat and training centers that they need, and usually they do not have the facilities that the religious communities can dispose of.

Then, there are all the adjustments necessary in order to keep up with the many relocations and requirements that the great mobility of the present population impose on superiors and subjects. Not only are our own institutions expanding at an enormous rate, but every sector of the Church is calling for help and at the same time professional requirements are increasing and are putting addditional burdens, both financial and personal-wise, upon our communities. This is asceticism at its best. It is really suffering with the Church its growing pains, its problem of readjustment or adaptation and also its internal evolution.

And the parishes are clamoring for aid in the training of lay teachers, in the youth apostolate and in the care of the children who are being educated in the public schools. You may be sure that the programs of religious education will be ever more expanded as our schools will have to turn away more and more children unable to find room in our schools. While we are educating 600,000 young people in our Catholic high schools, 1,600,000 Catholic boys and girls are frequenting public high schools and often not because they want to, but because they have to. The Church is becoming increasingly more concerned for the teen-ager and the religious education of adults — adult education through study clubs. Religious education outside the framework of our educational institutions is being organized, and again, the facilities and the personnel of our institutions are needed. It is easy to say, leave it to the layman, but the layman needs to be formed spiritually and apostolically. There is no doubt but that we, as religious, will find ourselves more and more involved in this kind of religious and apostolic formation. Communities should be open to this kind of apostolate which may not be provided for by rules or constitutions and yet the Church is calling for it. This means living in the rhythm of the Church and it requires considerable asceticism, expenditure of time and energy. Asceticism can easily move in this direction.

II. THE MISSIONARY APOSTOLATE OF THE CHURCH

As members of a religious community we must be attached to the total mission of the Church, the total mission of salvation. There are no apostles except through the Church, and for the Church. This attachment to the Church is manifested and fulfilled by our insertion into the visible structure of the Church, by our active submission to the hierarchy. This sense of the Church orients apostolic aspirations. It is not a matter of wishing and promoting the success of our work, of our movement, of our community and thereby of ourselves. It is a matter of entering into the plans of the Church and of promoting her success. Sometimes the apostle will have to sacrifice all actual success in preparing for the future success of the Church. Charles de Foucauld, for example, had to renounce the apostolic success of the present in order to prepare the framework for a work that is having its repercussions today throughout the world, not merely in the persons of the Little Brothers and Sisters of Jesus, but in the awareness of the duty to become a witness to Christ in the midst of suffering mankind. Similarly the case of Father Paul of Graymoor, preparing the work of reunion, is in place here.

This way of seeing things permits a more lively experiencing of the solidarity that binds apostles in common work. No one can undertake anything alone; it is the work of men linked together, the work of an organism. No one in the organism can be disregarded; each one is of service to all for the common effort. All those who within the Church concur in one way or another in maintaining the hierarchy and the sacramental order, concur by that very fact in the common salvation. Also, the law of apostolic success is not to seek to reap and count the fruits of personal success: "There is one who sows, and another who reaps, but all will rejoice in the work accomplished together" (John 4:36-37). "Paul planted, Apollos watered, God gave the increase."

This insertion in the Church not only touches our *exterior activity*, but our whole *spiritual life*. We live in the Church and for her, even to our most intimate prayers and sacrifices. We accept the fact that the rhythm of our prayer and of our penances passes through her structures, as well as those of our own action. But that is not a constraint for the Christian, because his vocation calls him to live in the Church, so that by this very insertion he discovers that for which he is made. In the Church and in the Church alone his prayer reaches its fullness in the liturgical mystery; his suffering finds its meaning in rejoining that of the Mystical Body; just as his action ends by being inserted into a Catholic structure. It is there that he lives, that he breathes and fulfills himself completely. And without doubt that is not accomplished without renouncing his tastes and his particular aims, but this very submission, by detaching prayer and action from their own caprice, this paradoxically *permits* their full liberty in the pure gift of self to the designs of the Father.

We must develop *a sacramental spirit*. By this we mean that we must not only center our life upon the great sacrament of Christ, which is the Church, but on the way to attain full membership in the Church and this is achieved through this mysterious incorporation into the Mystical Body of Christ through the sacramental action. Routine and ritualism have done their havoc here, too.

The Liturgy is stripping our religious attitudes of their formalism. According to Father Hofinger, the most serious obstacle to Christian living today is "formalism," going through the rites, the ritual without realizing what is happening. "A deep sleep induced by following a routine, mechanical set of operations and jobs, without a realization of the vitality and urgency of really living with God. We are so busy with superficial things, we work only on the periphery of life, so that we can't begin to live in the important things. We are lost in a maze of gadgets and just don't know what is important."

We must not merely partake of the sacraments in order to benefit by them. We must develop a deep spirit of faith which disposes the soul to receive them and to make them operative. Baptism and Confirmation and Holy Orders are sacraments that we receive once, but their effectiveness is permanent, assured by the seal of Christ, the character that endures. Through Baptism we are constituted children of God. Through Confirmation we have become adults in Christ and the grace of the sacrament is there continually effective in its function provided we allow it to operate. We must be aware of two dangers with respect to the sacraments, expecting them to be automatic signs of Catholicity, or taking them for granted as handy things to receive but not more necessary than an occasional solace or relief in time of need. As a matter of fact, it is God's way of inserting us into the

Mystical Body of Christ and this gradual transformation is precisely the job of these mysterious realities provided we do not put obstacles in the way of Christ's actions. How often did not Christ ask during His lifetime: "Dost thou believe?" All things are possible for those who believe. "Have faith; thy faith hath made thee whole." Christ's action in the sacraments is precisely of the same effectiveness — dependent on our spirit of faith, a living faith which tries to do everything in one's power to bring the most perfect dispositions to the sacraments. This means that we try to live our Christian vocation as a dedicated state and surely the dedication of the religious life can be a marvelous framework for this. Also we live out our Confirmation through involvement in our apostolate. Our daily apostolate has the character of a sacrament provided we bring to it the fidelity and sincerity and wholeheartedness that a professional job requires. The sacrament of Confirmation is the grace that is at work when we witness for Christ as nurses, as teachers, as social workers, as administrators. Let us not disassociate the maturity of the Christian with the daily run of duties of our state in life. Our apostolic life is a sacramental life. Through it the grace of Confirmation is brought into action, continuing the work of Christ and of the Church through us. Our professional duties are really the Church exercising her apostolate. Asceticism is called for to render that professional task the best ever and we can have the assurance that we shall not know here and now the consequences of that act of service we are performing.

Our personal contribution is needed for the Sacrifice of the Mass. Through this mystery, Christ has effected a union between Himself and our contribution, the contribution of His membership. Whatever the Catechism has about the Mass being the unbloody renewal of Calvary is true. But it generally glosses over the important contribution that the people are making to the sacrifice. The offertory is their offering and it represents the work and the service and the daily immersion into the world of men that our professional existence represents. What is so little emphasized is the unity that is achieved at Consecration between Christ and His membership when through the words of consecration Christ makes the offering His own. He changes His membership into Himself; He incorporates it into Himself to bring us divinized to His heavenly Father at the moment of the little elevation. *"Per ipsum et in ipso et cum ipso."* Then we have every right to call God our Father, as we do, *"Pater Noster."* The Mystical Body is essentially established at its fullness through sacrifice of the Mass and yet we must know that Christ expects us to make a perfect offering of ourselves and everything we represent by way of teaching, nursing, administrating, as social workers, or whatever capacity we occupy in the framework of salvation.

III.   Christ-the-King Spirituality

The consequence of all this is that we have a very important function to perform in the Mystical Body. We must prepare the world for its sanctification. We can do this in several ways. First obviously we must be witnesses to Christ, as we have said so often already. Our work must preach Christ, not so much by mouth as by example in that we perform the best kind of occupational competence. This already grows out of our status as a citizen of God's kingdom, still more out of our religious dedication. But we can also seek to influence the world that we represent in a Christian way by trying to set it aright. We can't do this alone, unaided, but surely there are opportunities where our authority in the professional field will command respect, where the example we give as an institution will make people sit up and take notice. I don't mean that we have to advertise ourselves, but we must show the professional world that we represent what the proper course of action should be to make for a sane and Christian way of life. Let us not hide our light under a bushel. The Catholic Church at this juncture of our American history is coming into a position of being heard. It is through our institutions that we are members of the professional world. Let us show the way of wisdom. And again, by that I do not mean that we have this all blueprinted. It means that we have to work with others in discovering the solutions to the problems. We have supernatural lights to guide us but this does not excuse us from working out human solutions and human answers to the problems that plague the world. This we religious have to do and when we do this as teachers, as nurses and as administrators, then we shall also come close to them and their personal problems. The temporal order brings us together so that through the common problems we can also communicate something of the deeper life and the higher ideals that alone can save humanity.

IV.   Liturgical Awareness

This large conception of life is what I would call the liturgical spirit. Everything that we see around us is a sign that speaks to us of God. The student must discover God through discovering reality, through getting to know the physical reality in biology, the social reality, the metaphysical reality. God does not have to be mentioned at all and yet we are closer to God by the very fact that we know God's creation better and have come to discover something that reflects the Creator's presence. The same is true of all our works and of all our striving. It is God who is present everywhere and we gradually become aware of it. Of course, sometimes we would like the help of the sacred writer and sing the praises of God through the psalms or through the prayers of the Church. The orientation of this prayer is toward God, not toward self.

And, too, the modern phenomenon of biblical revival helps us to see the meaning of the Church better. The Old Testament is nothing but a symbolic reflection of the Church, and the New Testament is nothing but the historical roots of the same mysterious reality. It would seem that at last the Church is in a position to do today what it should have done at the time of the Protestant revolt, but at that time the Church in the person of its members was not ready for the challenge that the Protestant revolt posed for it. Because we Catholics are gradually emphasizing the interior Catholicism and the community values that they strove to arrive at without the Church, the present moment is very propitious for a reunion of Christendom. Instead of emphasizing what separates us, let us give more thought to the many things that we have in common; then the Protestants will see the gaps that need still to be filled in their religious pattern. But the hour is here and let us help the cause of reunion by meeting them not on a religious level so much as on a professional level. On that level we can speak a similar language and after all in this pluralistic society of ours we are in touch with the non-Catholic at every turn, except on a Church level.

CONCLUSION

Living the rhythm of the Church does not complicate life. It marvelously simplifies it. It is what we are dedicated to and the Church is our means of salvation in every sense of the term. The Church exercises her apostolate through us; she commissions us to be her representative, her mouthpiece, her miracle worker, her doctor and teacher, her guide and counselor. All these functions we carry out for her provided we also speak her message truly and with a single mind.

In the first conference we said that modern society tends to be frank and straightforward in its general preference. The Church asks us to be good teachers, good hospital people, good social workers. Be really, truly what you are already. The modern society demands of its people love of initiative and vigor. This we have every opportunity to do. We have tremendous opportunities for courageous action. What we need is to develop human personalities, well integrated and accustomed to responsibility. The modern world is socially conscious. We are living a life of dedication and there is nothing more dedicated in this life than to be all things to all men, all within the framework of our professional competence. The modern world is democratic and respectful of human personalities. True charity, an effective community, is the best climate for the development of human personalities.

There is nothing we have to be ashamed of in our state of life. There is nothing that needs to be adapted, to be abandoned, to fit the pattern of modern society *provided* we live in the rhythm of the Church. The Church is calling for just such members and they are her sons and daughters continuing the work of salvation in this twentieth century.

SUGGESTED READINGS

KARL ADAM, *Christ Our Brother*. Macmillan, 210 pp. $3.00.
Seven historical and dogmatic essays on the life of Christ by one of the greatest theologians of the twentieth century.

KARL ADAM, *The Spirit of Catholicism*. Macmillan, 237 pp. $3.00.
A summary of the foundation of Catholic belief demonstrating the Church to be the organ of Christ's mediation between God and man.

LOUIS BOUYER, *The Paschal Mystery*. Regnery, 347 pp. $5.00.
A welcome presentation of the beautiful liturgy of Holy Week.

EUGENE BOYLAN, O.C.R., *This Tremendous Lover*. Newman, 345 pp. $3.00.
The author points out that every member of the Mystical Body is called to an intimate union with God in his soul. He then analyzes what this union means and what specific steps must be taken to develop it.

JOSEPH BUCKLEY, S.M., *Christian Design for Sex*. Fides, 216 pp. $3.50.
Exact theological principles concerning Purity, Modesty, Passions, Marriage and Virginity.

JEAN-BAPTIST CHAUTARD, O.C.R., *The Soul of the Apostolate*. Gethsemani, 290 pp. $2.00.
"Catholic Action must have as its preliminary the individual sanctification of each of its members, so that the supernatural life abounds and superabounds within them" (Pope Pius XI). Although written primarily for priests, this deeply penetrating book is equally useful to the lay apostle. The rule that prayer is the foundation, the *soul* of the apostolate applies to every follower of Christ.

JEAN DANIELOU, *The Salvation of the Nations*. Sheed & Ward, 118 pp. $2.00.
A searching book on the missionary problem facing the Church in its attempt to Christianize the world.

DANIEL-ROPS, *Saint Paul: Apostle of Nations.* Fides, 163 pp. $2.75.
A beautiful, fast moving, popular biography of the man who worked out Christ's command in the earliest days of Christianity.

F. DESPLANQUES, *Living the Mass.* Newman, 180 pp. $2.75.
A penetrating, prayerful paraphrase of the Mass intended to integrate the Holy Sacrifice into all the acts of our daily life.

EVA FIRKEL, *Woman in the Modern World.* Fides, 211 pp. $3.50.
Discussion of the human, physical and psychological nature of woman and the vital issues which face her.

ROGER HASSEVELDT, *The Church a Divine Mystery.* Fides, 263 pp. $4.50.
A complete doctrinal explanation of the Church from its beginnings in the Old Testament to its final fulfillments in the Heavenly Jerusalem.

CLIFFORD HOWELL, S.J., *Of Sacraments and Sacrifice.* Liturgical Press, 183 pp. $.90.
An account of the work of our redemption under the aspect of its continuation and application through the liturgy.

EDWARD LEEN, C.S.Sp., *What is Education.* Sheed & Ward, 288 pp. $3.00.
What modern education ought to accomplish as explained by an accomplished scholar who is one of the greatest spiritual writers of our age.

LOUIS LOCHET, *Son of the Church.* Fides, 255 pp. $4.50.
Activity in the Church, purification in the Church, contemplation in the Church — these are the three themes that recur. Engaging in the Church requires purification of our energies and that leads to contemplation.

P. MARIE-EUGENE, O.C.D., *I Want to See God* (Vol. I) and *I Am a Daughter of the Church* (Vol. 2). Fides, 575 and 696 pp. $5.75 and $6.75.
Throughout both volumes of this synthesis of Carmelite spirituality, the author uses the rich writings of St. Teresa of Avila, St. John of the Cross, and St. Therese of the Child Jesus.

PETER-THOMAS ROHRBACH, O.C.D., *Conversation with Christ: An Introduction to Mental Prayers.* Fides, 171 pp. $3.75.
This easy to follow handbook is an introduction to mental prayer based on the five steps of St. Teresa of Avila.

MARY PERKINS RYAN, *The Psalms* and *Key to the Psalms.* Fides, 306 and 188 pp. $3.95 and $3.50.
A clear, modern translation of "God's Songs" and enlightening notes for those who would enter more fully into the psalm spirit.

CESLAUS SPICQ, O.P., *The Mystery of Godliness.* Fides, 183 pp. $3.50.
A commentary on the three pastoral epistles of St. Paul, treating of the apostolate, preaching, and the priestly piety.

SUPERIOR-SUBJECT RELATIONSHIP

IN VIEW OF

THE PERSONAL DEVELOPMENT OF THE SISTER
Parts I - III

Reverend Charles J. Corcoran, C.S.C.

~~~~~

I

The Superior and the Ends of the Community

My work with that of Mother Rose Elizabeth is to discuss our general theme in terms of the "art" of the superior. But I want to stress most particularly the spiritual side of your endeavor, and to explain a little the principles which will enable you to grow and to share with those with whom you live and work the benefits of your development. When I asked, in the early part of last winter, what were the topics assigned to me, I was told that the Sisters themselves had expressed a desire to hear something about the personal development of the superior, something about her impact upon the house over which she is placed, and finally, something about her role as a counsellor and advisor. My first topic is the personal development of the superior.

The superior is primarily a spiritual guide and leader, not an administrator. She is appointed as the head of a religious house made up of women who are dedicated by vow to the pursuit of perfection. She is placed over the house of a religious community, whose end is, above all, spiritual. Primarily and most fundamentally, the superior operates in a spiritual milieu. Because of her presumed talents and virtues she has been appointed to this post; but here we come face to face with a paradox. Is it not strange that in this era of specialization the only persons

Note: These lectures were delivered from outline and are here published with minor corrections, as tape recorded.

who are not trained for their position are superiors? At least I have never come across an institute that had a house to which were assigned the men and women who at graduation were to take charge of some house. If there were such a house it probably would be called an "institution," and there would be a high wall around it — not so much to keep the populace out as to keep the inmates in.

It is a paradox that those who are entrusted with such a tremendous mission have to acquire the *savoir faire,* the art, by themselves. It is a paradox that the development of the superior is, under the present circumstances at least, a question of "in-service" training. It is not necessary for me to elaborate in any way the necessity for a development on the part of the superior, the necessity of this "in-service training," of this personal, individual growth and development.

There are two very self-evident principles which establish this necessity, and they are really two expressions of one fundamental truth. As a person is, so does he act. If I am worldly-minded, my actions, my thoughts, will be worldly, as well as my reactions to situations. If I am spiritually-minded, if this is my cast of intellect, I am going to think in terms of the eternal and I am going to judge things, as the spiritual writers say, *sub specie aeternitatis* — under the aspect of eternal values. This is completely evident. It is also evident that if I want to give somebody something, I have to have it in my possession beforehand. I cannot give what I do not possess. So when you apply this to our particular context it is evident that if the superior is primarily the spiritual guide and leader of her community, then she herself must be a spiritual person. If she is not a spiritual person, she is not going to act in a spiritual way. She may mouth spiritual principles, but there will not be that sincerity, that conviction, which alone makes one's pronouncements acceptable.

Similarly if she herself has not a breadth of view she is not going to be able to give the inspiration and the help that her Sisters have a right to expect from her. Is it not true that so often we complain that this superior or that superior is not catholic in her thinking; catholic — that is to say — universal, or broad enough? It happens too often that a Sister who has been, let us say, in education work for the greater part of her religious life will have very little empathy, very little understanding of the apostolate of the hospital, or of the social mission. It is difficult for this person to see all of the problems entailed in the work of the Sister-nurse, the hospital administrator, the social worker. Unless she makes a real effort to acquire this breadth of view, she is not going to be able to give to those who are not professionally her own type, the leadership that they have the right to demand of her.

So you see the necessity for "in-service training"; the acquisition of a real spiritual mentality is of the very essence.

What I would like to stress for you is particularly this: First: the goal of this "in-service training." We say that the superior is the spiritual guide and must develop herself in order to attain that efficiency and competency which will enable her to carry out her task. That is her goal. But I wish to explore this a little more with you, and when I have finished, I want to draw your attention to means which will help the superior to attain his goal.

The goal of the training, of the personal development of the superior is competency, competency as a spiritual guide or leader. As I said previously, the superior is primarily at the head of a religious house — *religious* house — therefore, at the head of a group of women dedicated to the pursuit of the spiritual life. When we think in terms of the superior in this way we are all, theoretically, convinced that first of all she must give the inspiration and the help that will aid her fellow religious, her Sisters, to attaind the end of the community. But that is where the difficulty begins: the end of the community. In substance the constitutions of all institutes, whether they are orders or congregations, are the same. As a matter of fact the Church has a model constitution to which all documents must conform before approval. The constitutions say: the "general" end of the congregation or institute is the glory of God through the sanctification of the individual members. The "special" end is the apostolate, the apostolate of education, the apostolate of foreign missions, the apostolate of the care for the poor sick, the apostolate of social work, and so on. You have there, in your document, two ends set up — a general end and a special end. The special end characterizes this institute and sets it aside from others. But all of us, as religious, have one and the same goal: the glorification of Our Lord through our own personal sanctification. I submit that this is not as well understood as it should be. There is a certain ambiguity, or at least an ambivalence, in the use of the word "end" as we find it in these documents. Certainly the person who is well informed will not find this ambiguity, but until he is well informed he might make some very fundamental errors in appraising the purpose of the institute.

When we talk about a *special* "end" are we really talking about an "end"? An end as a goal, an end as the purpose for which a thing exists, or towards which it is operating, is a good that is sought. Is the apostolate the ultimate good? Is the spreading of the Kingdom of God among our fellow men the purpose for the existence of our community? Yes and no. The ambiguity! The ambivalence!

The apostolate, we must always remember, is a means — not an end in the strictest sense of the word. We have an apostolate; we teach or we take care of the sick, or we do social work, or we go into the foreign missions in order that working through this particular apostolate we may glorify God. The apostolate then, the special end of the community, in reality is a means to an end. If we understand that then we will have removed the first possible misinterpretation and source of ambiguity.

Now certainly you religious know that, for I have stressed something that is very obvious. But I wonder if you have paid enough attention to the full import of that other end, which we call the general end. Do you realize that in that concept there are really two concepts? When we say that the general end of the community is the glorification of God through the sanctification of the members, we are talking, if you will permit the academic terminology, of an ultimate general end. This is the end-all of our existence as religious. But what is the proximate end — what, immediately, is the end of the community?

The end of the community as the community — that is what we forget. The end of the community as a community is to establish the milieu, the environment, in which its members may work out their sanctification for the glory of God. That is why the community is constituted as a society, in order that there may be the climate, the environment, the milieu, call it what you will, in which virtue can grow, the milieu in which the individual religious will acquire that virtue without which they cannot reach perfection and cannot therefore glorify God as religious. Besides establishing this ideal environment the community also purposes to give to the members the means which will enable them to profit by the milieu and the environment. That is the purpose for the existence of the Congregation of Holy Cross; that is the purpose for the existence of the Sisters of Notre Dame; of this Institute, of Dominicans, or of Ursulines, and so on. That is why we exist as a community.

If this is true, then the primary purpose of the superior is to establish within her own household the milieu and the environment necessary for the development of virtue. It is the superior's prime responsibility to see that her Sisters are provided with all of the means at the disposal of the community for their individual advancement.

I said that it is my experience that this truth is not understood. I would modify that. I do not think it is understood in the practical order. Certainly all of us have gone through a postulate, a novitiate, and years of training in a scholasticate before we were sent out on the missions, or before we priests were ordained. During those years of study this truth, explained now in this way — now in that, was drawn to our attention. We religious understand the theory, but I do not think we understand the practice, because it has been my experience that when it is a question of the government of a house the local superior is under tremendous pressure to meet certain standards of accreditation, to provide for a certain number of Sisters for a certain definitely assigned number of tasks. This pressure comes from without, it comes from pastors — the local pastor and the chief pastor of the diocese — it comes from parents. The pressure that makes the superior think in terms of qualitative changes and perhaps quantitative changes, too, is a pressure that comes from accrediting agencies. But all these pressures are brought to bear upon a woman who has at her disposal perhaps only a handful of subjects. Besides these exterior pressures she is under pressure from within; from within the ranks of her own subjects, but above all from the conviction that every day has just a few less hours than its predecessor, and the hours themselves a diminishing number of minutes. There is, in other words, before this superior the problem of administration, the problem of providing for the material welfare of the house and its well-being, its good order. The pressure to provide the Sisters with the necessary training, the pressure to meet the demands of the public. And these pressures are of such a nature and are so insistent that they do, in effect, too often stultify the theoretic conviction that the primary purpose of this house is the sanctification of the individual members through the practice of the religious virtues and the employment of the means that the community has assigned as the way in which the environment for the development can be attained.

I have a profound conviction that religious all over the world are very definitely threatened and tempted by the heresy of action. Most particularly, with a Pelagian cast. The heresy of action is this: the feeling that, whatever may be the theory, what we have to do is to staff this school; what we have to do is provide this community with a hospital of 150 beds; train administrators, not to mention superintendents for the different floors and departments. In a word, the apostolate becomes the end-all of the house's existence. That is, to erect a means into an end. And no matter what I may feel about the theory, if, in effect, I so act, then I am guilty, in the practical order, of the heresy of action. It is not only the heresy of action that concerns me, but the heresy of action with a Pelagian cast. You remember from your Church history the heresy of Pelagius. Pelagius maintained that it is possible for man to reach his perfection, and indeed to reach eternal happiness, by employing his own natural resources. This principle denies the necessity of grace, at least the necessity of internal grace such as we understand it. The Pelagians felt that if man takes advantage of the different means put at his disposal, he can without any intervention on the part of Almighty God develop himself to the full and attain eternal happiness. Is it not true that, in effect, too often the local superior will so arrange the prayer-life of the house that it becomes, for all practical purposes, a formality to be squeezed in between occupations devoted to the apostolate? Is it not too often true that the Sisters are not provided with the leisure and with the peace necessary for the development of an interior life? If these things are not provided for, it must be for either of two reasons: either because the person does not believe that they are of primary importance, or, if she believes that they are of primary importance, she has not the courage to put first things first. I said at the beginning, and now by way of conclusion at this point, I repeat: the goal of the superior's "in-service training," the purpose for this personal development of the superior, is competency as a spiritual guide and unless there is conviction there will be no development.

The second point to which I would draw your attention is this: the superior must be aware that the primary means for the attainment of this goal are her faith and a sense of responsibility. You cannot have any real growth and development unless it is an organic growth and development. In other words, it must be a development or growth of life. Now what is life? I am not a scientist. I am not even a philosopher, but I do know that the philosophers and the scientists agree more or less on a nominal notion or definition of life. They describe life as the ability to move one's self. In other words, they speak about life as being manifested by the power of inner movement. There is a rock. I can move the rock. I can push it. It cannot move itself. It has no life. But suppose that at a sufficiently early hour of the day and when I am completely in command of myself, I look at the rock and see it moving. I would correctly conclude that my rock was in reality a turtle. I thought it was a rock; it looked like one. In reality it was not. It was something living because it had the power to move itself. And that is what the philosophers call by a technical term: immanent activity — that is, the power to act which arises from within the being. So the superior's growth must spring from an inner principle of an intellectual nature. I cannot desire anything, unless first I know it. I must know something about an object before I can be drawn to it, before I can direct my activities towards its attainment. The word we are seeking is *conviction*. I must be convinced that I will not attain my goal unless I put into practice what I know theoretically to be true. And how will I get this conviction? What will nourish this conviction? Faith. We are concerned with a supernatural activity. If it is a supernatural activity, then it must be founded on and directed by supernatural knowledge. I must be guided in all my endeavors by the supernatural truths that Almighty God has revealed to us and which Holy Mother Church infallibly interprets for us. But this faith, which is the source of conviction, in turn will be active, and dynamic, only to the extent that it is nourished by a genuine spirit of prayer. Why? The answer is in the nature of prayer.

What is prayer? Prayer is speaking to God. It is the conversation of the child with its Father. When I pray I come into personal conscious contact with the God who is within me, the God who is all around me, with the God in whom I live and move and have my being. It is when I speak to God that I realize that He is here, because I know I cannot carry on a conversation with someone absent. Conversation presupposes mutual endeavor. It is not a monologue, but a dialogue. It takes two to make a conversation. So I can really pray only on condition that I am conscious of His Presence and listening to hear Him speak to me. Indeed the sacraments, my participation in the liturgical prayer of the Church, will not be ultimately effective unless I have prepared myself for their full value by this conscious, intimate association with God.

The second means which will bring out this conviction is a sense of personal responsibility. We must never forget that basic to the whole Gospel of Our Lord Jesus Christ is the Parable on the Talents. The purpose of our existence is to glorify God. The Redemption made it possible for us once more to give glory to God. The Church was established in order to facilitate our glorification of God. That is our end: the end of our creaturehood. And God the Creator made us individuals. He gave to each one of us a certain amount of talent, certain qualities, certain potentialities and possibilities. It is through the exploitation of these possibilities and these potentialities that we are to glorify God. Hence, if I have a sense of responsibility I will realize that as I am a composite, not only of soul and body but also of the temporal and spiritual, I will glorify God to the extent that I perfect my human nature and supernaturalize it and bring it to full fruition. Only the person who does this will be fully able to develop. So this consciousness of personal responsibility is the necessary complement of the prayer which nourishes faith. If the superior avails herself of these two you may be sure she will have fashioned herself under grace into an instrument which Almighty God will use in His own way and His own good time for the sanctification of her fellow religious.

II

The Impact of the Local Superior on Her Community

All of us had, at one time or another, the duty to commit to memory certain dates of history. And probably we were told that there were some ten or twelve dates that singled out the most momentous events in the history of the world, of the history of the United States, or of the Western World, and so on. One of those dates, without doubt, is October 14, 1066, the day of the Battle of Hastings. Hastings was, in reality, one of the pivotal events of the world, certainly one of the most important dates in the history of the English speaking world. You remember the circumstances. Harold the Fair, the successor of King Edward the Confessor, St. Edward, had during his very brief reign, the task of preserving the England that had come to him as his inheritance from the invasions that came from the Norsemen and the threatened invasion from the Normans across the Channel. He had a valiant army at his disposal; a high-spirited group of men, well trained and well officered. But he also had two wars to fight. First of all he had to thrust back the Norsemen — and he did, at the decisive battle of Stamford Bridge. There the invaders from Scandinavia were routed and England was free from their threat. But just at that moment, from the East came word that William of Normandy was about to launch the invasion which had been threatening for many months.

It was necessary, therefore, for the tired veterans of Stamford Bridge, to turn now and go over towards the sea and to defend England from the horde that was coming across the Channel. These men had already fought a hard fight. They were victorious, but they were victorious at the cost of a tremendous number of fallen, at the cost of a vast loss of material. They were tired, and though they were victorious they were dispirited because the rumors that came across the Channel told of a tremendous number of soldiers, well-equipped, fresh, and inspired with a desire to conquer new lands for their leader. This was the situation that confronted Harold the Fair as he considered the strategy for this which everyone realized was to be decisive for the future of his country. Material he could not provide the men; recruits were not forthcoming. Weary veterans would have to bear the brunt. In an endeavor to make his force, such as it was, as powerful and potentially victorious as possible he called upon a certain Bishop Wulfstan to address the soldiers on the eve of the battle. Hope Munz in her novel, *The Golden Warrior,* describes the scene. The bishop gathered the men around him, and though, as the author said, he had the gift of words, no man had ever heard him speak as he spoke this night. And he chose not his own words, but he used the thoughts of the fathers of his nation as he set forth the wisdom, the holiness and the beauty garnered in England from Augustine's time. And it seemed to each man as he listened that, for the first time, he saw his heritage. Because they had been inspired by the eloquence of Wulfstan these soldiers, poor in materiel, poor in number, went out the next day and fought valiantly, and literally to the last man. But they were overwhelmed and victory was given to William, henceforth to be known as "the Conqueror." Still those Anglo-Saxon soldiers who died on the field of Hastings are venerated as among the great heroes of the world. Here were men who fought against tremendous odds, fought valiantly and in their own way victoriously, because the traditions of British valor were as much of their making as of any of their predecessors or successors.

My dear Sisters, we too are in possession of a tremendous tradition and heritage. That heritage and tradition is perhaps, on occasion, set before us by an eloquent speaker; at other times we capture it in the documents and histories of our institute. In any case we know our tradition, and from it we derive much of our present strength. The wisdom, the beauty, the holiness of those who went before us is handed down to us. From them, our forebears in the congregation, we receive not only our name, but our responsibility. Tradition is not merely a matter of heritage; it engenders in its recipients grave responsibility. Tradition, if it is true, is a vital, growing factor as it passes from generation to generation, and as it passes from hand to hand it garners new riches; the principles of the past, the beauty and the holiness and the wisdom are enhanced by the addition of the wisdom and the beauty and the holiness of the present. *Noblesse oblige!* We must live up to the traditions and to the history of our community.

Now it is the local superiors who, before Almighty God, have the prime responsibility to preserve that tradition. As someone has said, it is the leader who is "the custodian of the people's memory." It is the superior's duty to receive the tradition from the past, interpret it, declare it, set it forth, and then in her turn control it as it passes from her com-

munity to those who are to come after. She is not only the custodian of
past memories, but also the shaper of the here and now. Our community
is composed of living members. It is an incarnate reality. Our constitutions set forth the shape of our community; they determine who may be
elected to this office and what are the prerogatives of that office-holder.
But it is the living members of this generation who determine who is to
hold the office of superior, who, in other words, is to be primarily responsible for tradition and for the present.

Our communities, if they are of any size whatsoever, are composed
of small units. Our religious do not live simultaneously under one great
roof, or in one large house. They are separated into different local communities. It is here, in this particular geographic spot, that the community exists. It is now at this moment that the community exists. There
was a community of the past. The community of today is here and exists
at this moment. And so, my dear Sisters, it behooves us, at a moment
like this when we are thinking in terms of the responsibility of the superi-
or, to reflect very seriously on the duty of this officer to see that the
community here and now is as perfect, as wise and holy, and beautiful
to behold, as possible. It is the local superior, even more than the provincial superior or the superior general, who gives the tone to the community, because it is she who must take the law, i.e., the rules and constitutions, and apply them to the here and now. She is not a legislator
in the strict sense of the word. For that matter, neither is the superior
general, since the making of laws is the prerogative of the General Chapter for the community as a whole and of the Provincial Chapter for the
province. Nevertheless, it is the local superior who takes those laws and
as executive interprets and puts them into force. Similarly she is not a
judge in the meaning of Canon Law; she is not to establish juridical
processes and pass sentence on miscreants. But it is for her to correct, and
if necessary to punish within the limits of her competency. The local
superior, therefore, is the incarnation of the community's authority here
and now. This being so, I should like to draw your attention particularly
to four areas in which this responsibility must be met.

The four fields are the fields of Worldiness, of Prayer, of Obedience,
and finally, of Poverty.

I do not think that time will permit me to explore, even superficially,
all of these fields; but I should like to draw your especial attention at
this moment to the one which I think is the most important, namely,
that of Prayer.

Previously I drew attention to the fact that the superior of a religious
group is not primarily an administrator. She is an administrator, of

course, but her most important role is that of leader of her fellow religious in the ways of God. It is the superior who is to stimulate the inner life of her community.

I also drew to your attention the fact that it is in prayer that the superior strengthens her convictions. It is in the light of prayer that the superior sees what is to be done at the same time that she recognizes her own selfishness and shortcomings. It is likewise from prayer that the members of the community associated with her will derive their force and their power.

Now in the community we have public official prayers. Just as the Mystical Body of Christ, the prolongation down through the centuries of Jesus, the Redeemer, the King, the Priest and the Teacher, has its public prayer, its official prayer in the liturgy, so too our organizations which in their own way too are organisms, living, palpitating bodies, have their public official prayer, their liturgy, namely, the exercises of piety. You perhaps will remember that St. Pius X in his famous *Motu Proprio* on the liturgy, published at the very beginning of his reign, says that the liturgy is "the prime and indispensable source of the Christian spirit." It is as we pray the liturgy and because we pray the liturgy that we will be the Catholics we should be. Similarly too, the liturgy of the community exercises is the prime and indispensable source of our religious spirit. When I pray as a religious I do not come forth to pray as Charles Joseph Corcoran; I do that when I pray privately. When I pray as a religious I pray as a religious of Holy Cross, as a son of Moreau. I pray with a new dignity added to my own unworthiness. I may have charity, limited though it may be. I may have a sincere desire to better myself. I may really feel inspired to adore and worship God in the form of praise; and all of that will be laudable. But if I praise and adore God as a religious; if I beseech Almighty God for certain favors as a religious; if I, in company with my fellow religious, ask His pardon not only for my own sins but the sins of my fellow religious, then that prayer of mine has a power and an efficacy that it can never derive from my own private virtue or dignity. Now if this is true, you can see where the responsibility of the local superior lies in regard to the prayer-life of her subjects, because it is the superior who not only presides over the exercises, but who must likewise see that they are well made.

At this moment I envisage two hypothetical situations which can confront a local superior. The first hypothesis is this: by reason of the traditions of the community and the grants of the constitution the local superior has a very large discretionary power in regard to the determination of the timing, the spacing, and the other details of the exercises.

She must do this, of course, within the framework of the constitutions and the traditions, and the order of day which she draws up will certainly have to be submitted to the approval of the major superiors. This understood, however, she is allowed to determine when and where and how the prayers of community are to be said. When this hypothesis is realized, the local superior must see to it that the optimum of silence and leisure is provided to the Sisters, because these are the two indispensable conditions for *good* prayer. And before I go on further, let us remember that we are talking about prayer — not about recitations, not about the rote repetition of certain formulae, but about prayer. That is to say we are talking about those moments when we, as a corporate entity, come together with one mind and heart to praise God. And because we are to pray vocally, that is by employing formulae that have already been determined, we will pray to the extent that we mean what we say. If we do not make those words our own; if we do not use these words as the vehicle of our own interior dispositions, these formulae will be formulae, beautifully phrased perhaps — but not prayer. That is why I said the superior must provide for silence and leisure.

Silence means, in the negative sense, the absence of those external noises and disturbances which make concentration difficult; positively it is the atmosphere of calm and peace. The leisure we are speaking about here means time from which are excluded those inner pressures which preclude a calm consideration of the things of God. Such pressures result as often as not from the feeling that time not devoted to external works of charity is time wasted. The opposite of course is true. Joseph Pieper makes the point most forcefully in his essay *Leisure, the Basis of Culture*. Leisure he correctly defines as time given over exclusively to meditation and reflection on the things of the spirit.

Hence, the silence and leisure about which we are speaking cannot be understood merely in a material sense. The superior, indeed, may enforce the law of silence. She will see that there are no unnecessary noises or disturbances in the house at the time of prayer. That is to provide material silence, but she knows that this is but the external element of silence. She is conscious that silence in the fullest sense of the word is something in the soul itself. It is that peace and calm of which we spoke. It is that absence of distraction and preoccupation which Our Lord figuratively spoke of as retiring into one's closet and closing the door on all that is not God. It is true that over this inner silence, the real, important silence, the superior has no immediate control, for it is the responsibility of each individual religious. But what the superior can do and must do is to provide the circumstances and the conditions under which this silence of the soul may prevail. The same remarks apply to leisure with the necessary modifications.

In the hypothesis where the superior has been given discretionary power for the timing of the exercises and so on, I say that the superior must realize that she is not going to provide the silence and the leisure necessary for prayer, if, in a silent house, she squeezes the exercises in between other operations and other occupations, which of themselves are destined to preoccupy the practitioner. I know of cases where religious women who have been working in the classroom are asked, during the 45-minute lunch period, to take their luncheon, say the beads, and make their Particular Examen. Leisure? Silence? Well, there is no one around talking to them. If they are lucky they may have found a closet to which the clamor from the playground does not penetrate. But is that the silence, is that the leisure, which the Sisters have a right to demand if they are going to recollect themselves? Notice the word that the spiritual writers use: recollect — pull oneself together and address oneself seriously to God.

When we are asked to literally jam in certain prayers, because there happens to be fifteen minutes available, can our superiors reasonably expect us to pray *attente, digne ac devote* — worthily, attentively and undistractedly?

The superior then who would have the power to determine when and where and how the exercises are to be conducted should be aware of her responsibility to see that these exercises are placed at such a time in the day when, reasonably speaking, the religious are in a condition to address themselves to God. When are these periods? Certainly—early in the morning, before the burden of the day must be assumed, and the heat. Late afternoon, again, when the work is over and there is at least a brief period of physical rest. Finally, in the early evening. But it is not my task to speak in terms of these practical details. Fortunately I can remain in the realm of principles. But the person who in my hypothesis would have the opportunity to so arrange the exercises of the community and would not remember that prayers are something more than recitations but communications with Almighty God which demand silence and leisure, such a person would have much to answer for before the Throne of Almighty God.

I come to the second hypothesis which, I suppose, is the one most likely to be verified in the case of the majority of you here present. I envisage now, not a local superior who has been granted this broad discretionary power, but who has been told that though the school day is very full or the hours on the ward very many, nevertheless there must be two meditations every day, common spiritual reading, common recitation of the Rosary with all the trimmings. There must also be, perhaps, the Chaplet of the Blessed Sacrament or the Dolors of Our Lady or the Chaplet of St. Joseph. And then, in the more idle moments of the day there are to be at least two of the Hours of the Office chanted in public. Have I exaggerated? Perhaps a little bit.

I do not have to remind you how crowded your day is with religious exercises. And you know, too, how in many instances you are not free to determine when they are to be held or whether they can be curtailed or altogether omitted. You have received a mandate; it is your duty to carry it out. What can you do under these circumstances, in this hypothesis? What is your responsibility in regard to the prayer-life of your Sisters? It is perfectly evident that your prime responsibility is to make the best of a sorry situation: that goes without saying. And that, if silence and leisure are the indispensable conditions for community prayer, then to the best of your ability you must assign or you must give or provide for as much silence and leisure as possible. That goes also without saying. But what can you do about it? You can remember this: you are the superiors of your respective institutes. As superiors you form its governing body. If you are not ex-officio members of all the Chapters, at least your voice is a potent one and one to which the community must listen.

Consequently I submit that you are bound to do everything in your power to see that the prayer-life of your community is made reasonable if it is unreasonable. I say *if* it is unreasonable; *if* it needs reform; *if* it needs revision.

I am seriously presuming some adjustment is indicated. Perhaps you know that at the present time the Holy See is preparing a thorough revision of the Divine Office to meet the exigencies of the priests' life in this feverish world. We priests are bound under the pain of mortal sin to recite the Divine Office every day, and under the pain of venial sin to see that we *pray* this Office. That means we are obliged to an hour or an hour and a half of vocal prayer. But the breviary as it exists today is of monastic origin and inspiration. The seven canonical Hours were devised by the monks of centuries and centuries ago. In many instances the length of the Office and its particular form were designed not merely for the praise of God, but also for the penance of the monks who could be chanting it in choir. What was suitable hundreds of years ago for a group of semicontemplatives is hardly adapted to our present form of life. The Holy See recognizes this and so has undertaken a revision of the Office. When it will be promulgated we do not know, but we all hope it will be soon. And it is significant that the liturgiologists usually speak about this revision as a reform. Now if Holy Mother the Church sees the need of adapting the prayer-life of the priest to the pressures and circumstances of the present day, is it too much for a religious to hope that the authorities in his community will revise the Directory prayers, the exercises of the community, so that they will be more reasonably apportioned throughout the day and adapted to the circumstances and the pressures of our American life?

And so, in the second hypothesis, as a local superior you can endeavor by every means at your disposal to bring your prayer-life into conformity with the day that is ours. Just as the breviary, historically speaking, is of monastic origin and has a monastic complexion, so too the exercises of most of our communities were determined in a France of a hundred, two hundred, three hundred years ago when the schools were small and private. If they were parochial institutions there were not very many pupils. If they were private institutions they were academies or colleges. And the same is true if your origins go back to the Germany of fifty or a hundred years ago. Most of us come from communities that had their origin in Europe and the prayer-life of the community envisaged that milieu and that era. Things have changed. Certainly our founders did not envisage the vast and complex parochial establishments we have today. I do not think our forebears knew about accrediting agencies and the demands that they make on us. And because theirs was a more leisurely life, a more confined life, they could assign exercises to certain times of the day with the assurance that the necessary silence and leisure would obtain. We could prolong this discussion ad infinitum, but I think that I have made my point.

I have used my time in speaking about the impact of the local superior on her community, in this single area of Prayer. What I have said applies equally to her responsibility to keep the world out of the community, to preserve the law of cloister, for the here and the now. It is the responsibility of the local superior to see that obedience to the higher superiors is real and warm and religious. It is from her own sense of obedience that the religious under her care will derive to a great extent their appreciation of obedience. And the same thing for poverty. But I did specialize on this matter of prayer, because whether we are teachers, nurses, social workers, administrators, or what will you, we are primarily religious. We are therefore persons consecrated to the worship and service of God. Yesterday and today I have emphasized the spiritual reality of this vocation because, as I said yesterday and I repeat today, under the pressures of work we too often forget the first things. And so, you who are the custodians of your communities' memories are likewise the shapers of its present and the architects of its future. Yours is the responsibility. The community will be what it is if your impact on it is salutary. Or, I should say, the community will be what it should be if your impact on it is salutary; the impact of a spiritual person concerned above all with the inner life of herself and her subjects.

Aspects of Religious Authority:
The Local Superior as Counsellor

I want first to clarify my use of the word *Counsellor* in this present context. Modern psychologists clearly distinguish between counselling, guidance, instruction, and spiritual direction. My fellow panelist, Father Curran, has clearly indicated their respective functions. When I use the term "counselling" I borrow it from the vocabulary, not of the psychologist or the educator, but of the spiritual writer. In this sense it is simply synonomous with spiritual direction.

Now spiritual direction is understood as the help given one in view of personal sanctification and perfection. It envisages therefore something more than the attainment and maintenance of the state of grace; the possession, therefore, of the state of union with God and all the panoply of virtues and gifts which this state entails. Spiritual direction envisages the fulfillment of one's potentialities. It is therefore a broader and richer concept than that of the state of grace.

This help may be of different kinds. It may be in the form of instruction as to the nature of the spiritual life, its means, methods and so on, or it may be in the form of exhortation, advice, correction, stimulation, what you will. Thus the word "help" is taken in a very broad and comprehensive sense, and direction itself is understood as a generic term. As there are different kinds of help, so are there different species of direction.

First of all there is *pastoral* direction. Pastoral direction is that given in public to a group. Its subject matter, of course, is the spiritual life, but the manner in which it is treated is impersonal. It is called "pastoral" because in the organization of the Church it is the pastor who is immediately charged with the responsibility of the spiritual welfare of his flock. And so, anyone who has the equivalent position of a pastor, a religious superior for instance, when he or she gives a public exhortation or an address on the spiritual life, is said to be giving pastoral direction. So too the conference master who comes to the convent every month; *a fortiori,* the retreat master, and so on. Pastoral direction — public direction, direction given to a group.

Then the spiritual writers discuss *sacramental* direction. Sacramental direction is that which is given in the confessional and on the occasion of the administration of the sacrament of Penance. Ordinarily the priest will given an exhortation to the penitent, will encourage him to use such and such means to better his spiritual life, and so on. Sometimes you hear this exhortation referred to as a *ferverino*.

Ordinarily speaking, the sacramental direction will take its inspiration from the confession of the penitent. Hence it particularly envisages the problems and difficulties we encounter in our struggle to purify ourselves. Needless to say, however, it can also be quite positive in tone.

Finally they discuss *spiritual* direction. Taking the word spiritual in a highly technical sense, spiritual direction in this technical sense is understood as that help which is given habitually to an individual as an individual. It is distinguished, therefore, first of all from pastoral direction, insofar as the recipient is not a group, but a person, an individual and the proffering of help is not given in public or through public means but in a very individualized, personal contact. It is distinguished from sacramental direction insofar as, ordinarily speaking, it would be given outside the sacrament or at least certainly not necessarily in connection with it. Do not misunderstand me. Spiritual direction, in the sense that I am talking about it now can be given and perhaps ordinarily is given to nuns on the occasion of the weekly confession, but it takes place after confession is completed. Thus spiritual direction is an individualized, personal relationship. Furthermore there is the connotation that this relationship is a habitual one.

If we want to grasp the full significance of this relationship, let us define the spiritual director as the one who aids another to discover and understand God's designs in his behalf and assists him in realizing these designs. You see this definition or concept is much more profound, much richer, than the one which simply says that the spiritual director is one who helps another habitually in the matter of spiritual perfection.

God's designs. Every single one of us, my dear Sisters, is an individual. We are created by Almighty God as distinct and separate from everyone else. And since God creates ultimately for His own glory, each single one of us is destined to give God a measure of glory, a kind of glory that no one else who has ever lived or who ever shall live can give Him. In that sense God has for each single soul a design. Our dignity is to realize a detail in this providential plan for the universe. The spiritual director attempts to help his directee find out what his potentialities reveal as God's designs in his behalf. We must study our powers, talents, gifts; we must be made aware of our shortcomings, our habitual faults, in order that exploiting the one and correcting the other we may attain to this tremendous dignity of a true individual glorifier of God.

The director envisages Charles or Mary or William or Agnes; but Charles, or Mary or William or Agnes as he or she exists here and now; here in this institute, in this congregation, as a member of this religious family. Now, not in the generation of the director himself, not in generations to come, but at this moment. This individual is to give glory to God through the full development of his potentialities. The director helps the directee discover and understand this primary fact.

Then he undertakes to assist the soul to realize this destiny. How does the assistance take place? It may be that what is needed most of all is instruction at a given moment. Or it can happen that exhortation and stimulation is the requisite. But all of this in view of helping the individual live his vocation. He needs help because none of us, as we have heard hundreds and thousands of times, is a good judge in his own regard. We are blinded by the mere fact that we are examining ourselves. There will be, therefore, a subjective cast to many of our judgments; and if we are going to be prudent, we will seek, therefore, the help of someone who presumably, at least, will be objective in viewing the situation. It may be that the directee lacks the courage to begin the work because he fears that success is impossible. An objective judge would assure him that it can, indeed, with God's grace, measure up to the ideals and with persevering help attain them.

There is a final word. The director *aids*. He aids the directee whose responsibility it is to develop. "No matter how tall your father is, you must do your own growing," say the Irish. But the director can help, and his help is given exclusively to this one person according to his needs. For this reason I find most felicitous the expression of the school of Dr. Carl Rogers, "Client-centered Guidance."

But that is not all. The director is an instrument in the hands of the Holy Spirit, the first Director of each one of us. In this sense the director helps God, the Spirit of Truth and Light. Perhaps you remember the title of one of Bishop Sheen's books, *Three To Get Married* — the bride, the groom, and God. Three for direction: the directee, the director and God.

Now by the very nature of things the person most competent to give this direction is the priest. First by reason of his training. He has been trained in dogmatic, moral and spiritual theology. Presumably therefore he knows not only the principles involved but also the practical means and devices that are going to help. He has been educated precisely for the purpose of helping souls to attain to the fullness of their creaturehood.

But not only by reason of his education is he competent. The priest is competent, too, by reason of the fact that he has been ordained by Almighty God for just such a purpose. The sacrament of Holy Orders imprints upon him a character which designates him as a spiritual leader in the Church of God. When the priest is ordained he receives the Power of the Keys, the authority to forgive or to withhold forgiveness of sin. All the moralists, theologians, and spiritual writers are unanimous in interpreting the Power of the Keys to mean something more than is implied in the administration to the sacrament of Penance. They understand it to embrace the whole of the spiritual life. As a matter of fact, the traditional way in which theology speaks about the role of the confessor indicates that. We say that the confessor is not merely a judge, a *judex,* one who is to determine whether or not forgiveness is to be given to the culprit, but also a *doctor,* a teacher, and a *medicus,* a physician. Threefold is his role as confessor: to forgive if he judges forgiveness in order; to teach the things of God; to help as a kind physician repair the damages that sin, personal and original, has brought to the soul.

There cannot be any question, then, as to who, given the very nature of things, is the most logical and constant director. But, by the very nature of things, the religious superior is also competent. Let us not forget that. By the very nature of things. What are the things whose nature indicates this competency? First of all, the superior is competent as a religious. The superior is a member of the same family as the subject to whom she would be giving this help. Both of them have been educated and raised in the same ideal. That ideal is substantially the same in every religious institute, but there are nuances, emphases, peculiar to each institute. The superior knows those ideals because she has lived them herself. She has received instruction; she has received counsel. She knows from practice what is the particular type of religious virtue that the Dominican Sisters, or the Sisters of the Holy Cross, or the Maryknoll Sisters want in their subjects. As a religious she is living in daily contact with her subject. Therefore she can see, she can observe, she can sense. She is in a position to know whether or not the one coming to her for help is in possession of that fundamental spirit that should characterize a religious of their institute. She is in a position to know the ideals, to know the person, and consequently to put the two together in view of aiding her fellow religious attain the fulfillment of the designs of God. As a religious she can give spiritual counsel.

In the second place she is particularly competent as a religious superior. We call her a superior — that is to say, the one who is elevated. You may not like the term; I don't. But, in any case, the leader, the one who is responsible for the care of the house is, in the Church's concept, on a higher level. If we must think of elevation let us talk about it insofar as the vantage point from which the leader may see more than a person down on the ground.

As head of the house the superior controls certain sources of information which the ordinary religious does not possess. Take the case of a young religious. If a Sister is transferred from one house to another, presumably some sort of record will be sent to the new superior, telling of the Sister's success in other employment, her potentialities, and very probably certain defects of character and so on. The superior has in that dossier information independent of any she might acquire from consulting the Sister herself, or from her own personal observations. Then too the written record will be supplemented by remarks of former superiors and associates. From her position as superior, she derives definite competency.

In the third place she is competent as a woman. There is one thing that is quite sure, I believe, and I believe all psychologists agree on this point: that we understand our own much better than those of the opposite sex. Men understand men better. And women understand women better. Of course, a priest should never say that because we are supposed to be exhorting and instructing and solving your problems. But any priest who has a modicum of common sense knows his knowledge of women is not perfect. And so, as a woman dealing with another woman, the religious superior has a peculiar and special competence.

And finally, let us hope in most instances there will be another source of competency, namely her personal qualities and experience. I don't think it is open to question that a superior has a very definite competency in this matter of direction as we have defined it. But that competency is definitely limited and circumscribed.

In the first place it is limited by reason of the office that she occupies. Just as that office gives her a special vantage point, so does it limit her direct responsibility to the external government of her house. The Church insists that the superior, whether priest, Brother, or Sister, keep out of what we call the "internal forum." The superior, *qua* superior, is formally forbidden by Canon Law to delve into matters of conscience. From this derives the first limitation on the superior. But, on the other hand, if the subject spontaneously wishes to discuss matters of conscience, certainly the superior no less than anyone else may listen and give counsel. And the second limitation comes from the fact that, ordinarily speaking, even the most experienced Sisters will not have sufficient professional training in matters of conscience to give the final counsel or the ultimate instruction in a given case. That is why the superior who knows her responsibilities as well as her limitations, after having given such counsel as she feels is indicated, will refer the individual to a priest who can delve beneath the surface and who, as director and/or confessor, can discuss matters of conscience with all right and propriety. Hence, while we admit her competency, we must also admit her limitations.

But this does not mean that the superior has not a genuine responsibility in regard to the interior life of her subjects. Remember, she is not primarily an administrator but the leader of a religious house; that is to say, the leader of a group of religious dedicated to a common goal of self-sanctification and perfection. And consequently, granted that her canonical competency is in the external forum, does that mean she cannot be helpful in a more intimate role? Our Blessed Lord told us, "By their fruits ye shall know them." We can learn much from examining the fruit. Though she may not delve beneath the surface she may make some very sure and shrewd judgments.

Let us now consider two practical problems. First, how should the superior act when subjects want to consult a priest for direction? That they have the liberty to do so is self-evident. The religious comes to the community to attain perfection. The Church, therefore, insists that when it is a question of our perfection we enjoy very considerable freedom. Here we are concerned only with direction, not with confession.

Now certainly it is conceivable that at times a request for direction would be unreasonable. But how are we to decide this? I presume, of course, that we are dealing with normal individuals, not with psychotics or even serious neurotics.

I would say that there are two criteria. Unreasonableness as regards the timing. Spiritual writers tell us that if we wish to facilitate our advance in the spiritual life we should seek the help of a spiritual director. Naturally one would ask immediately: how often should a person go to direction? You will find a variety of answers, of course. But, ordinarily speaking, I think that they would agree on this as a norm: in the case of young religious, particularly those still in the process of formation, a monthly consultation is indicated. For older religious, those who have formed and who have acquired some practical experience, such frequent consultation is not necessary. For them perhaps a quarterly consultation would be sufficient. The superior, therefore, using these norms, could judge a Sister unreasonable who would say, "I want to go to direction every week." It could be very well that in an individual case there would be special reason for such frequency, but ordinarily that will not be true.

Therefore if a Sister would ask to consult a director every week or every ten days, the superior quite legitimately I think, could protest.

Second, unreasonableness in the choice of the director. I have had some experience with these unreasonable demands. Sister Mary likes Father William as a director. But Father William is in the East. Here at hand are Peter, Paul, James, Andrew; all competent, all willing to help. If William is to have the privilege of giving this favored soul favored treatment he will have to be summoned from afar or Sister will have to be given the necessary means of transportation to betake herself to him. Is it reasonable? It could be, under special circumstances. Ordinarily speaking, a request of that kind is not reasonable. And therefore, that would be another criterion for a legitimate refusal. In conclusion let me cite a concrete case. A group of our priests had been preaching in one of the Eastern states. It had been a successful mission and the Fathers were just preparing to leave the rectory when a little old lady came rushing up to the door and said: "I want to see Father Smith." When Father Smith was produced, she whispered, "I want to go to confession." So over they went to church, and Father Smith heard her confession. When he rejoined his companions and was about to leave the little old lady came running down the stairs and poked her head in the car. "Thank God," she said, "now I've gone to all of ye." I submit, from personal experience, that some religious have an analogous ambition. If you suspect that Sister X is like that, I think you could quite reasonably tell her to consult one of the priests who habitually come to the convent for that purpose.

I want to say one final word about another problem, secrecy. And the word is very brief because the principle is so clear. Secrecy is demanded of the superior who has been the recipient of the confidences of a Sister in the course of direction. I am thinking most especially of those circumstances where the subject will have manifested some problems of conscience to the superior. The superior has an obligation to the community to see that all of its members are worthy members. Would the superior be obliged to inform the major superiors of a subject's unworthiness if she knew this unworthiness only as a result of a manifestation of conscience? Or put it this way: can she, under any circumstances, reveal such matter, or use it herself in her official capacity? Let us first define some terms. Subject matter of this kind would fall under what the scholars call a "professional secret." A secret is noncommunicable knowledge. It is called a *natural* secret if the reason why it is not communicable comes from the natural law. I know, for instance, that John and Mary are not validly married. I am the only one who knows that. John and Mary, though they have done wrong, have a right to their reputation. Therefore, by reason of the natural law, my lips are sealed and I cannot manifest this knowledge that I have. Then there is the *promised* secret. "Did you know that I'm going to be changed? Mother General has accepted a new mission over in Fort Wayne and I'm going to be the first superior. Now don't tell anybody. You promise, don't you?" You see, if a request for secrecy is made after the revelation then the technicians say that it is a promised secret and would bind the person only under terms of fidelity, and there would be plenty of reasons why, in certain circumstances, the person, though he had given his word, could be released from it. Finally we distinguish the *committed* or the *entrusted* secret. Here the obligation of secrecy precedes the revelation itself. In other words, a person would not reveal this matter to another unless it were understood to be a privileged communication. Ordinarily this committed secret is an implicit contract. In other words, a person does not have to say, "Now I'm going to tell you something on this condition." It is certainly implicit in certain relationships that we call professional relationships: doctor-patient; lawyer-client; superior-subject; director-directee. Because there are professional relationships, the incommunicable knowledge resulting therefrom is known as a professional secret.

There are innumerable problems which arise in any discussion of professional secrecy. An excellent scientific disquisition on this subject can be found in Father Regan's book, published some fifteen years ago, *Professional Secrecy in the Light of Moral Problems.*

I am not concerned here with the general principles; much less with the exceptions when professional secrecy could be broken, and so on. What I want to draw your attention to is this, that in the unanimous opinion of moralists and canonists and spiritual authorities, the secrecy implied in this relationship of direction, by whomever the direction is given is a professional secret, and as such is so privileged that under no circumstances can it be violated. In other words, there are never any circumstances — never *any* circumstances — when a superior who has received a manifestation of conscience of a subject should reveal, or can reveal, that matter. This secrecy is considered by the same authorities to be second only to that sacred secrecy of the confessional. No priest could reveal what he heard, no matter what harm could be warded off from the Church thereby. Similarly, even to prevent a great harm to the community a superior cannot manifest what she has learned in a manifestation of conscience. The subject can release the superior, it is true, just as the penitent can release his confessor. But it is not prudent to ask your subject to release you, any more than it would be for a confessor to make that request of his penitent. What you can and must do is to try to convince your subject that she has a grave obligation to make her condition known. To your arguments you must add the most potent means of all: prayer. Prayer that God will give her the courage to do what is right. You can talk to God and to your Sister, but in the presence of all others your lips are sealed. You must trust that God, in His Divine Providence, will take care of the community if you remain mute. Theologians draw our attention to the fact that here there is a conflict of two goods. On the one hand there is the good of the community which would be compromised by your silence; on the other hand stands the good of what we call the institution of direction itself. Now they all agree that in this circumstance, the good of the institution of direction takes precedence. Why? Because if it were known that a director, at least under certain circumstances, would communicate his knowledge, then the confidence of the people in the institution of direction would be compromised, if not totally lost. This good, therefore, in the mind of all these authorities, takes precedence over the good that the manifestation might bring about in an individual case.

Now I conclude these conferences by returning to the first words with which I began them. The superior in a religious institute is not primarily the administrator of a house but the leader of her fellow religious in the ways of God.

The impact that she has on her house is incalculable. She sets the tone. The individual local superior sets that tone for her house; another superior for another. But let us remember the wise conclusion of one of the great Greek philosophers: from many different tones comes the most beautiful tune.

Not only must she be aware of this impact that, in the Providence of God, she is to have on her fellow religious, but she is also to remember that in the Providence of God she is set in this house to help the others in their spiritual problems insofar as she is competent to do so and with the limitations about which we have spoken. If the superior realizes these truths, then she will have contributed mightily to the good of her community and to the advancement of the cause of God here on earth.

SUPERIOR-SUBJECT RELATIONSHIP

IN VIEW OF

THE PERSONAL DEVELOPMENT OF THE SISTER
Parts IV - VI

Mother Rose Elizabeth, C.S.C.

IV

Personal Development of a Superior

Speaking of a superior's personal development, Father Charles Corcoran has stressed her role in the congregation's organization. He showed the need for her to grow in holiness and the importance of her constant striving for deep inner perfection. Father emphasized the fact that only by God's grace, assisted by human prudence and common sense which should come with experience, can a superior hope to save her own soul and assist those entrusted to her to save theirs.

In short, Father Corcoran, following St. Thomas, pointed out that a wise superior, in order to preserve her sense of values, chooses the proper means to the right end.

My task is to give you some specific illustrations of these principles Father has spoken about — things I have learned the hard way in one office after another, about the superior-subject relationship and the self-mastery it demands of the superior as well as of the subject. But to save time and to give more point to my examples, let me preface this talk with some commonplace but pertinent remarks about the local superior. I know all too well that, amid the piecemeal day-by-day emergencies that arise in all religious institutes, superiors cannot give to their office all the time and effort it deserves. Therefore, important considerations are often unfortunately overlooked in the daily struggle. Some of these considerations are:

1. If the congregation is to realize its aims, the local superior
   has unique importance.

2. She receives only haphazard training for her responsible position.

3. In any religious congregation, she is the "key man" and needs the key virtue of prudence if she is to function adequately.

When more than two human beings are banded together for a common purpose, they need a leader who will see to it that their objective is gained. He must steer the group between two extremes — that of unrestrained individualism on the one hand and exaggerated conformity on the other. While the group is small, confined to a single location and absorbed in one work, a single leader will suffice. But let the group begin to grow and the leader is immediately confronted by the law of diminishing returns unless he shares his growing burdens with others. The law becomes more demanding, as the organization increases and takes on new works. To maintain good order in any activity, conformity is necessary. Nevertheless deterioration often sets in when individualism is sacrificed completely. In the struggle to preserve at the same time both good order and individual rights, every organization of any degree of complexity develops a bureaucracy and a hierarchy.

Religious congregations, as all of us are painfully aware, are not exempt from these societal commonplaces. In fact, they have a special poignancy for us. A large business firm or a government strives constantly to preserve individualism because that necessary dynamism is lost when everybody is reduced to a number on a file card. Initiative, new ideas, progressive thinking are likewise lost. But for a religious order, because we are linked together through a common bond of religious life, the injury is much greater. *Our* reason for protecting the individual is this: Each soul has a sovereign importance in God's eyes. Furthermore, the primary objective of any religious congregation is the sanctification of *each* member.

The superior general is ultimately the one who is responsible to see that this primary objective in religious life is fulfilled. And under her, the provincial superior is assigned this task. But if this work of such sovereign importance to the community is to be carried out effectively — if this objective and all other purposes as well are to be successfully attained — then the local superior who is united in charity with these Sisters approximately 365 days out of the year, is truly the one upon whom this constant task of formation depends.

The superior occupies the place, enjoys the opportunities, and has the responsibilities of that single leader of a group of more than two whom I mentioned a few minutes ago. It is quite plain, then, that a religious congregation, whether contemplative or active, will succeed in its primary objective (sanctification of the individual members) and its secondary objectives (good works for the Church and society) only to the extent to which it discovers good local superiors.

As a former Provincial and a former Mother General, permit me to pause and underline that statement. Even more than the mistress of novices or the junior mistress, the local superior is the cardinal officer in the congregation's hierarchy. She is as vital to the work of a congregation as are the noncommissioned officers in the armed forces or the permanent undersecretaries in government. Neither the generals and admirals in the one case, nor the President and his cabinet in the other, no matter how brilliant they are, could be effective unless the officers immediately responsible for the implementation of policy were capable of grasping that policy and communicating it to their subordinates and enlisting their subordinates' efforts in carrying it into effect.

It might be well here to repeat those three things:

First: The local superior must have the mentality to grasp the community's policy. She should be steeped in her community's way of viewing things. She does not decide issues according to her own special background or ideas. Rather, she thinks, "What is the Holy Cross way of solving this problem?" or "Is this the Mercy solution, St. Joseph, or Franciscan solution?" "What does the community do in cases like this?"

Second: The local superior must not only have the spirit herself, but must also have the ability to communicate this spirit to her household. For the Sisters, she represents their dearest love on earth, their religious family. When someone from another house steps in the door, the visitor should be able to say, "This is truly a Holy Cross convent." "This is the Mercy, St. Joseph, or Franciscan convent," or "I knew I was 'home' right away." The local superior spreads the community spirit throughout her domain, so that her Sisters, too, in their smaller fields, give off the fragrance of their own community's spirit. Let us not forget, however, that though each community has its own particular characteristics, all of them should reflect above all else the spirit of Christ.

Third: The local superior must enlist the cooperation of her subjects. I will not spend time on this point right now for it will be covered fully in the next talk of this series, Superior-Subject Relationships.

I hope it is sufficiently clear, then, that the local superior is the key person in our religious congregations. Higher superiors must work through her; subjects must work under her. She is the intermediary, the channel, the communication line between the Sisters in the ranks and their higher superiors. We know what could happen to a congregation if the local superior became an obstacle to the institution — a bottleneck, as it were.

Being placed in a superior's position is a challenge for even those confirmed in faith and who have seemingly "put on Christ." All one's powers — mind, will, memory, imagination, emotions, passions, and bodily energies are called into play at the same time. Very often the superior is called upon to make decisions at a moment's notice — decisions which may affect all the members of the institute and the entire Church. The cause of God's honor is often in her hands.

Yet, oddly enough, this key officer usually receives no special training for her work. She was a Sister yesterday; she is a superior today. The community — indeed, Canon Law — prescribes a novitiate to train lay women to become Sisters. Provincials and mothers general almost always serve an apprenticeship in administrative positions. But how often is the local superior put into her position with no preparation for it. The armed forces have their noncoms' schools; our government departments maintain a trained personnel in cardinal posts insofar as politics permit. A local superior, however, is tossed into a position of authority and is left to sink or swim. Like a landlubber cast into the sea, the best she can do is to go through the motions she has seen swimmers use. But it is one thing to sit on the sidelines and watch a good swimmer; quite another, to be in the water yourself. The local superior is fortunate if she has had the opportunity to watch an experienced superior in action and if she can enlist the interest and sympathetic understanding of her higher superiors.

A superior's assignment is not the work of angels but of men. It is a man-sized job. If it were not for sanctifying grace and the infused virtues that accompany the grace of Baptism, the only reliances one would have to fall back upon would be "guess and gamble." Even though Sisters have the grace of Baptism and have received the sacraments for many years and have kept their rule, have been good teachers or nurses, experience proves that many placed in authority without some training for the work do not know the best thing to do, nor how to do what must be done here and now for the greater good. Consequently we have all made our mistakes, and mistakes are costly. The help given a local superior can be expressed in such current phrases as "In-Service Training," "Playing by Ear," or "Do It Yourself."

Where shall we place the blame for this situation? Suffice it to say that societies of religious women are like all other organizations, ecclesiastical and lay, governmental and academic. They never have, at one time, enough administrative talent available to fill with ease and without misgivings *all* their administrative posts.

Since we have introduced the idea of comparing religious organizations with secular ones, let us see what means these other groups use to discover local executives. They employ talent scouts, for one thing, who ceaselessly scan the ranks. They use certain posts as proving grounds for positions of higher responsibility. Or, they set up formal training schools to develop certain kinds of leadership. In an emergency, when they need someone for a post of central importance, they will raid another organization and lure away one of its top men. We see that in baseball teams or in big business firms. This last device — fortunately or unfortunately — is not open to religious institutes.

The other means — talent scouts, proving posts, and training schools (more often, meetings or special retreats for local superiors) — may and are used regularly by religious congregations, to meet some of their administrative needs. It seems to me that the Spiritual Institute held annually at Notre Dame has done more than any other one factor I know of to train religious "in service" for the great responsibility their community places upon them. However, all superiors do not have the privilege of attending institutes; usually only after a superior has floundered around in the sea of authority for a time does she finally get any assistance for her difficult task. This is real In-Service Training, too, but the training is otherwise known as The School of Hard Knocks. It has its advantages to those who can benefit by them. Some of the best major superiors of every congregation are alumnae.

If a superior has "what it takes," as the saying goes, the newly appointed leader will prove on trial to have the combination of qualities of leadership desired. And if she has them and uses her talents rightly, she will inevitably bring to the surface whatever gifts for leadership might be latent in her. She will be an excellent talent scout herself during her few years in office. She will remember that the Church and her community are always looking for likely superior material, so she will, through her efforts, try to bring to light what there is of it in her own institute. A superior can best do this by being in close contact with each individual for whom she is responsible.

These techniques just mentioned may, at first, not seem practical to us. On reflection, however, we may find that they suggest many means that we might adapt to our needs. Right here I should like to emphasize an aid that I think would be most beneficial. Undoubtedly there are many communities that have this help. I speak of what might be called a special Handbook for Superiors. Such a guide would provide definite instructions and directives, the fruit of long experience, and would give to a new superior a sense of security and confidence in handling just those ordinary problems which she must constantly meet.

There are three virtues which should be the hallmark of every superior. The three are often intertwined; most virtues have a habit of twisting around each other until it is difficult for us nontheologians to pull them apart and thus catalog them in neat compartments. But these three combined make a good superior. They are obedience, loyalty, and prudence. And the greatest of these is prudence. Therefore I shall save it for the last virtue to be discussed.

Obedience is that virtue identified above all others with community life. Obedience holds a pre-eminent place in community living. Religious superiors, no less than their subjects, are bound by the vow of obedience. The Society of Jesus for four centuries has seen in obedience the principal means of forming a really spiritual person. The Jesuit, considering man as gifted with intelligence, places all his capacities at the service of obedience. "He must enter into the thought of his superior, and be concerned with what he has in view."

The most serious problem superiors must deal with is that of religious obedience. What would a superior say to a Sister assigned to teach the third grade if she refuses to be changed from the seventh grade because she felt it was a demotion? What if she refuses to take her turn presiding at the children's Mass on Sunday? Or objects to being assigned some duty in the convent? Or refuses to be changed to another mission? What would be the relationship that would be set up in such cases? St. Francis says that the truly obedient subject is not anxious to know where he is going. But if his superior sends him up to the loft, he must be careful not to arrive in the cellar. It is in the loft that he will find the will of God, manifested through obedience, and not through his own will.

If I single out the Jesuits and Franciscans in this matter, I do not wish to infer that they are the only ones who love and practice obedience. Our own Holy Cross priests and all others look to obedience as the very heart of the spiritual life.

The examples given above pertain to the obedience of subject to superior. The superior's obedience to her higher superiors will take the form, not so much of doing this or that as she is commanded, but — to quote the Jesuits once more — "to enter into the thought of her superior and be concerned with what she has in mind." This may be an example of such obedience:

A large missionary congregation of women has written in its directory a phrase tantamount to this: "Sisters are not expected to like publicity, still less to seek it. But they should realize that it is essential to the work of our congregation. We must make our work known if we are to gain support for it. Therefore, they should be considerate of representatives of the press and treat them with every courtesy."

It may be — and probably is — true that an individual superior might have a real aversion to publicity. She may even feel that there are better means of getting support for the congregation's mission work. She may have had experience with rude or inquisitive reporters. To her, newspaper publicity is "exaggerating one's own work," "puffing up one's accomplishments to ridiculous heights," "sprinkling tinsel on the pure gold of unseen work for God."

In spite of what a superior feels, however, she treats with every courtesy representatives of the press, sees that their legitimate questions are answered, and helps them to meet their deadlines. She is careful, however, not to permit publicity which lacks true dignity, for this would be to negate the purpose of the community's ruling, to gain support for its work. Such a superior is truly obedient. She has the mentality to grasp the community's policy. She has "entered into the thought of her superior."

Father Corcoran spoke also of *loyalty* in obedience. No doubt he abstracted this idea from the life of his holy founder. Father Moreau suffered so greatly from a lack of loyalty in some members of his congregation in the early days, that he never let pass an opportunity to stress loyalty. It is, he says, one of the first marks of a good religious. He warns his family of Holy Cross that they should never betray their brethren's weaknesses.

It might be well here to give an example of how this loyalty may be carried out in religious life. I recall a poor mission — a sanatorium situated in the heart of the desert. A superior was sent there who had none of the qualifications for this kind of work. She was a teacher and had never had any desire to be around sick people. The community assigned to her a young assistant who was capable, energetic, and a true apostle. She loved the poor suffering humanity who came to the sanatorium knowing they would probably not recover.

As time went on the young Sister had to take over more and more of the superior's duties. The superior, a very fine person, meanwhile had many side hobbies, which were far removed from the duties assigned her. One of these hobbies was painting pictures for poor churches. In the midst of the superior's absorption in a painting of St. Joseph, the young Sister, who had been unable to get decisions on numerous important items for weeks, went to her superior who was deeply absorbed in her art. She stated the case, posed problems, and recommended solutions. The superior seemed to be giving her undivided attention which pleased the assistant very much. The young Sister concluded by saying: "What are your decisions, Sister, concerning these matters? They require immediate attention." The superior looked thoughtful for a few seconds and then said, "Do you suppose I should put more paint on St. Joseph's shoe?"

The young Sister went back to her desk and continued to manage the sanatorium the best she knew how while the superior continued to paint pictures for poor churches. The loyalty in this story is that the community work was accomplished by someone other than the superior. The Sisters engaged in the work of the institute, as well as the patients and personnel, were unaware that the superior was unconsciously not fulfilling the obedience assigned her by higher superiors but kept on painting holy pictures while the young Sister was administering the superior's work to the best of her ability.

Although I am using this story as an example of loyalty to a superior, I can also state that this experience was not too good for a young Sister just starting out on her apostolate.

As for a superior's loyalty to the subject, let me tell you this story: The foundress of a most successful religious congregation — she died just a few years ago — appointed a young Sister as superior of a rather difficult house. The Sisters who were to be under her, were quite a bit older than she. They had entered in the early days of the congregation and had not received the thorough religious training later postulants received. But they all had good will and all had struggled valiantly in those early days to put the work on its feet. The Mother-Foundress spoke to the young superior the night before she left to take over her new charge. "You may find twenty-five different faults in each Sister," she said, "and all of them may seem to you to be quite glaring. But I want you to try to correct only one of these and forget the others completely. If you are with other superiors, never mention your troubles with any one of your Sisters. And with other members of the house, never speak of even one of these twenty-five faults you find in Sister So-and-so. So far as anyone inside or outside your house is concerned, you are in charge of good holy Sisters, which is the absolute truth. Then each one will be able to live her religious life according to the lights God has given to her."

It might be the place here to speak of a time when loyalty and the greater good of the individual and even of the congregation, seem to be in conflict. Prudence also enters into the picture. This may be the case when a Sister's conduct has necessitated her change from one house to another. The change is primarily for the Sister's spiritual betterment and secondly to restore peace and harmony to the house from which she is taken. Should provincial superiors inform the local superiors of the faults which caused the Sister's change? Would this violate justice and charity? On the other hand, if the local superior is not given some warning, may she not overlook or condone the beginnings of the same fault until it has again reached major proportions? Are not all communities familiar with the type of Sister of whom it is said, "She is fine the first year, troublesome the second, and impossible the third?" What about our loyalty in this case?

As to whether or not the local superior should be told, there are two factors to be considered. First, the nature of the Sister's fault, and secondly, the degree of prudence possessed by the local superior. Let it be said once and for all that should a local superior ever intimate to a subject that she has been "warned" in advance of her faults, that "The Provincial told me all about you," the whole foundation of the Sister's community life may be undermined; and the imprudence of the superior is worse than any possible fault the Sister may have committed.

If the local superior can be depended upon, not only never to reveal by so much as a lifted eyebrow what has been told her, but also not to let it prejudice her against the Sister, then it will be helpful to the Sister herself, to the Sisters with whom she lives and to the community as a whole, to have the local superior apprised of a *habitual* fault. She will then prudently avoid placing the Sister in the way of temptation. If priests are her "weakness," she will not be given charge of the sacristy, nor youth organizations which would bring her into contact with the clergy, nor placed in a remote classroom where "visitors" could go and come unobserved. Her correspondence will be firmly but unobtrusively controlled. In addition to these negative measures, the prudent superior will strive to keep in special touch with this Sister by confiding works to her which will bring them into contact.

If a Sister persistently indulges in particular friendships, it appears necessary that the local superior be told, at least in general terms, of this disposition, because she must guard against "coded" letters, clandestine intercourse by phone, letter and packages, and she must so assign the Sister to a duty where it will not be easy for her to establish a reprehensible relationship either with a companion, an employee, pupil, or parishioner. Again, extreme prudence is required of the superior. She should never, of herself, introduce the topic of particular friendships when talking privately with the Sister, nor make them the topic of her public admonitions. However, if she can by prayer, and patience and kindness get the Sister to open her heart to her and expose her dispositions, the battle is more than half won. But never, no matter what the disclosures, never must the superior express shock, nor even surprise.

Well, here we are — whether we wish it or not — already into a consideration of prudence. It is hard to discuss any virtue in relation to superiors, without plunging into prudence. It is the *sine qua non* for them. It is the "steering wheel of all virtues." Authority cannot be helpfully exercised without prudence.

If religious congregations have difficulty in finding good local superiors — and no doubt about it, they do — then the only solution to the difficulty is to spread prudence throughout the ranks. The local superior is the best one to do this. She is the cardinal officer and prudence is the cardinal virtue in what is otherwise a vicious circle. Prudence is an elusive virtue but so vital that, without it, a religious with every other qualification cannot be a good superior. As someone has said, "It is better to lack holiness than prudence." To decide at any given moment which course of action is most pleasing to God is a Herculean task. Yet the local superior must do this every moment of the day.

In trying to show what prudence is, it might be helpful first to say what it is not. Very definitely, prudence is not absolute certitude.

The superior who must always be absolutely certain before she does anything will end up either doing nothing or afflicted with an anxiety neurosis. As St. Thomas says, we simply cannot have, in things human, the certitude of metaphysics or mathematics. The lack of certitude, he says, makes one alert, quickens the faculties, helps one to see quickly into all the possibilities and, at the same time, to keep oneself on the watch. Mistakes are important. We must not think only in terms of success.

Right here it might be well to see how emotions fit into the framework of every life, even into the life of a superior. It might be well also, in trying to say what the virtue of prudence is *not,* to say a few words about the emotion of regret. Anyone who dares to attempt anything at all, at times makes mistakes. Mistakes should be valuable stepping stones to a better future. It is futile to try to change things that cannot be changed or to waste time worrying about the past. Mistakes are good tools with which to build a better future. For my own consolation I like to quote the following maxim:

> "For every evil under the sun
> There is a remedy or there is none;
> If there is one, try to find it,
> If there is none, never mind it."

This little quatrain makes a sound distinction between vain regret and useful regret which is helpful in making new decisions.

A superior would be a bigger person if she trusted more in Divine Providence and less in her own narrow vision. The story of St. Joseph and Our Lady, how they left their simple comfortable home in Nazareth to travel four days over rough country under most unfavorable conditions so as to fulfill a Roman edict, is a good example of acting without knowing all the answers.

Superiors have a special difficulty that is inherent in their office as superior. We are told that desire for power and prestige is something inborn in all of us to a greater or less degree. It is not prudent to take too much satisfaction out of the little attentions that Sisters shower upon them because of their office. Neither is it commendable for superiors to seek deference from outsiders. Unless one is careful she finds herself taking distinct pleasure and gratification in minutiae of office. We should strike the golden mean in this as in everything else and control these natural tendencies.

Now, what prudence *is*. It is defined simply, as "the habit of judging all actions with relation to the final goal of life." Prudence, as an intellectual virtue, does not tell us to be charitable, just and temperate. Charity may say to us, "Why not give that $20.00 you received, as a bonus to poor Mr. Wilson?" But prudence, calling on memory and past experience, and considering the greater good of Mr. Wilson, will say, "But Mr. Wilson is poor because he is a heavy drinker. It would be better to spend the money for groceries which would be delivered directly to his home and family."

Prudence spreads its wings over every moment of a busy day. Whether the superior is conferring with the bishop in regard to new works, or with the Sister-housekeeper about the next meal — at her desk, in her cell, in chapel, or visiting the classrooms — in relations with the pastor, the children, their parents, the employees and, most of all with her Sisters, she must exercise prudence. In celebrating feasts, observing fasts, planning bazaars, writing letters, or making potato salad, again prudence must come into play. Prudence is the "steering wheel," as I said before, which the superior must learn to handle if she does not expect to founder on extremes of all sorts. Let us see how prudence operates in various activities.

In financial matters, a prudent superior secures advice and counsel of upright, loyal, competent business or professional men. If debts must be contracted, she will look forward to how they may be paid. Now that most institutions have lay advisory boards, the advice of competent men and women may be had for the asking.

Prudence will regulate her zeal, so that she will not undertake works which the community cannot staff. The prudent superior knows that overwork is the rock on which many a religious life has foundered; first, physical health went, then the spiritual. A local superior will not introduce new courses into a school, or new departments into a hospital, before ascertaining how they can be carried on adequately from the viewpoint of both personnel and finance. She will keep constantly in mind "the heresy of good works" preached by Dom Chautard in *The Soul of the Apostolate* and she will not permit spiritual exercises to be omitted or abridged, save rarely and with her express permission. To what purpose are works expanded if the influence of the religious on those with whom they work is thinned and weakened? A prudent superior will never permit a Sister to be so involved with material and secular things, even under the guise of "good works," that she spends little time with the community and neglects recollection, silence and prayer.

To act prudently, a superior must use all the spiritual means at her disposal — Masses, prayer, recourse to the Holy Spirit, penance. When there is a doubt as to the proper means that should be used, counsel must be taken. After this, a superior must act and follow through with her decision.

This is often the crux of prudence, to follow through courageously on a decision. In the two stories which follow, the superior acted prudently and with courage. In the first story she saved a religious vocation; in the second, she saved her community from embarrassment and a girl from an unhappy life.

I heard a story not long ago about a girl who was graduated from a school of nursing. She asked the local superior to make application to the community for her. For three years of her training, she had stated quietly but steadfastly that she wished to be a Sister. But two schools of thought had developed amongst the Sisters. Some were very much in favor of her being received, and others were just as opposed to it. In the view of contradictory reports about the girl's disposition and temperament, the local superior was at a loss, and presented the case to the Mother Provincial, asking for counsel. It was evident that prejudice and passion, arch-enemies of prudence, were at work on both sides. Moreover, there was the girl's future as a Sister to be considered, if the question of her suitability could not be resolved. The provincial asked the girl to the motherhouse for an interview. She was invited to remain a week, with the explanation that she could thus get an idea of how the postulants and novices lived, and become familiar with the motherhouse environment. When a friendly relationship had been established between the provincial and the girl, the former led her tactfully to put the situation before her. The girl admitted that although she sensed the opposition of some Sisters, she did nothing to lessen it; on the contrary, she rather flagrantly showed how little she cared for their opinion. Being intelligent, she readily admitted her guilt in this matter, and soberly considered how it might affect her future in the community. When the provincial, after a number of kindly interviews, proposed that the girl work in a hospital operated by another community for a year and, in the meantime, keep in touch with her, the girl gratefully complied with the suggestion, for she had a deep and earnest desire to be a Sister. She worked with entire satisfaction as a staff nurse for a year. Then she again asked for admission to the first community. In the meantime, feelings concerning her had abated; in fact, some of the Sisters who had formerly opposed her admission, now rather feared that her thoughts would be turned elsewhere. The girl was admitted and, at the time this was related to me, had persevered happily for twenty years as a valuable and virtuous member of the community.

In the second case, the daughter of a prominent Catholic family, long time benefactors of the community, indicated during her high school days that she felt she had a religious vocation. Her family was delighted, and the parents' evident pleasure increased the daughter's determination to lead a religious life. However, her teachers noted that while she had a pleasing personality, her marks were below average, corresponding with what could be expected of an I.Q. of 78. They observed also, that when faced with a difficult assignment or an examination, she became morose, then resentful, projecting her failure on the assignment itself, the teacher's mode of making it, the distractions caused by her classmates, etc., etc. Despite this, the pastor joined with the parents in encouraging the girl to apply to the community. "It isn't fair not to give her a trial," was his stand.

The local superior felt that if the parents could be brought to a right attitude, the pastor would automatically be satisfied. The local superior invited them to talk the matter over with her. She pointed out to the parents that in the community more would be demanded of their daughter spiritually and intellectually than she was capable of doing. She said that the community's long experience proved that a Sister must find a certain satisfaction in her work, satisfaction derived from a sense of accomplishment and success. The girl had repeatedly demonstrated that she was unable to cope with difficulties. On the other hand, when she was not pressed nor brought into competition with others, she showed a sunny, happy disposition, and was eager to help others in those things which she could do well — things which had to do with manual skills — drawing, dressmaking, interior arrangement of drapes and furniture.

After several conferences (and much prayer on the part of the entire community) the parents began to see that their daughter's happiness was at stake. Not, as they had first supposed, would it be ensured by the community's accepting her, but rather by its not doing so. But there remained the hurdle of "What will her classmates, what will our neighbors *think?* We have told them, and so did our daughter, that she would be entering the convent as soon as she was graduated."

At this point the local superior suggested that the girl be transferred to a school in another city taught by a different community, a school that had an exceptional reputation for its Home Economics Department. The parents and the pastor both accepted this, as did also the girl. Removed from associations where she had to live up to her announced determination to become a nun, the girl found real satisfaction in developing her talents and shortly after graduating made a good Catholic marriage.

It has been said that the obedient Sister is the available Sister. I would like to say that the prudent superior also is the available superior. The prudent superior will be ready at all times to help the Sisters. She will try to have them see the authority of God in her authority, and she will distinguish between self and office. Someone in speaking recently to superiors said, "You who are superiors are obliged to do what you can to make every single Sister feel secure, accepted, wanted." And I would go a little further and say, "You are obliged to make them feel not only important but necessary."

The prudent superior will share her responsibilities with the Sisters and in this way she will make them feel that they are an integral part of the community and that her responsibilities are their responsibilities. Some time ago a priest expressed perfectly the point I am trying to make here. Permit me to quote from his letter: "In my first year of regency, the rector of my college called a faculty meeting shortly after school had opened. In it he laid before each of us the complete financial statement of that large and growing institution. He told us what money we had, what we could expect, and what we should spend. Then he went on to discuss the plans he had and the policy of the school. At that time, Mother, I was only twenty-three years old. I was young — but I was old enough to be a parent. Therefore I was old enough to know the business affairs of the house of which I was a part. Believe me, Mother, every member of that faculty left that meeting feeling that he was a member of the institution; that he had a place in the school, that he had a work to do for Christ and for the young men who would be under him in class, in the corridor, in the study halls, in the refectory, and even on campus. In other words, the running of that college was not left to the president alone. We all had part in it. I felt a member of a family, not just a number in an institution. And that has always been my ideal of the relations that should exist between superior and subject. We are all working for God. We are all striving for the spread of His kingdom. We must have someone who will issue commands, for God has stratified society and made His Church hierarchical, but a basic equality exists between members of an institute. Some superiors seem to think that they own the institute and the subjects are just allowed to work for them. No one is keener than youthful, independent Americans, whether in religion or out of it. They see through sham and stupidity almost immediately and they resent these faults and know they are an insult to God whom their superior represents." If we are dedicated religious, we shall be prudent religious. We shall see Christ in the subjects. Superiors will be convinced that the soul of each religious is vastly important to the work of God and His Church.

These are but a few — very few — instances of prudence. It would be quite impossible to give examples of the multifarious ways it shows itself in the comings and goings of a superior's day. In conclusion, then, let me give you one thought which may serve as a guide through that maze — your day —.

The religious should often reflect that prudence is the common trait of *all* the saints: not only of martyrs and bishops, but also of virgins and confessors. She will keep in mind that Christian prudence requires the sacrifice of material possessions in order to attain eternal treasures. She will seek to imitate her who is called "Virgin most prudent."

V

The Impact of the Superior on the Subject

Father Corcoran in his talk this morning on the superior's impact on the subject said that the religious life of each Sister is actualized *here and now* — here, in this house under the present superior, and now, according to her prescriptions for today. The sanctification of both superior and subject depends not only on what happened yesterday or what might happen tomorrow, but, what is more important, on what is being accomplished *now, here,* at the present moment. If we accept what Father says, then we believe that right here, *now* at Notre Dame University, under the golden dome of Our Lady, this moment is of vital importance to all of us.

Since my talk today deals with the superior-subject relationships, I would like to introduce this discussion by bringing in a question that Father Charles Connor, S.J. (a retreat master whom some of you may remember) used to ask his retreatants. Before each conference he would urge his retreatants to look in the mirror and say to themselves, "Oh, little girl of yesterday, what do you think of the girl of today?" Since most of us are superiors and, because the responsibility of superiorship weighs heavily and makes it necessary for us to spend much time helping others, we do not have sufficient time nor opportunity to study ourselves. It might be well during these days while we have the privilege of this Spiritual Institute, for us just to step aside and look at ourselves and see if we have grown from the little girls of yesterday to the spiritual stature of the valiant woman God wants us to be, and if we bear witness to the charity of Christ.

As an example of an ideal superior-subject relationship, I have taken a few ideas from the life of the Little Flower. St. Therese of Lisieux lived her life wholly dependent upon God; it was a joy, therefore, for her to cooperate with her superior, even though it demanded great effort on her part. With the eyes of faith she always saw God's will for her manifested in her superior. Such unselfish love which we find in the life of St. Therese is the only solid basis on which to build up a perfect relationship between a superior and her subjects. It was love, too, that made her superior able to reach out and help the Little Flower to achieve holiness, and it is only love that can draw out the inherent virtues that lie hidden away in religious souls. These virtues are there but the superior must find them. When superiors and subjects have a complete understanding of religious life and can meet on common ground, without either one losing any of her own individuality, both sharing in the divine life of love, then both superior and subject may be said to be functioning perfectly as parts of the Mystical Body of Christ. The soul of each Sister becomes a mirror in which there shines forth the resplendent image of Divine Glory. When such an ideal relationship exists between two persons that both are speaking the same language — the language of God, they have found in this relationship the secret of apostolic fruitfulness.

All of these points a superior may well study and meditate upon in considering her relationship with her subjects. Let us take each point and study it separately.

To Foster Mutual Love and Respect

The first is that of mutual respect and love. It is for both superior and subject to create a climate of sincerity and frankness when dealing with each other so that they may meet daily in a spirit of mutual charity. To do this both must practice humility and have the courage of their own convictions. To bring about a happy relationship, subjects must be trained and encouraged to express convictions without fear of an unfavorable reaction. The superior will lose none of her dignity when she permits her Sisters to express their opinions even though they differ from hers. And, if a superior wishes to have her Sisters grow and develop she should not consider every contrary opinion as a personal attack or a sign of ill will. On the contrary, she should be happy that Sisters are interested enough in the community in which they live to have opinions and that they feel free to express them. Spiritual directors tell us that there is a spirit of indifferentism in religious life today which is more dangerous than we realize. We are told that this attitude stems from a frustration on the part of religious when they are made to feel that they are not permitted to have an opinion. The superior shows great prudence when she gives the subject an opportunity to express herself as an individual. When young people come to a community they often seem to have much potential initiative and want to use it, but after a few months these same people find it hard to do even ordinary things. Where does the initiative go? What causes this sudden change in the Sister? Perhaps the answer is this. The new subject is so completely concerned with becoming a good religious and so convinced that she can have no independent thoughts that she instinctively believes that any personal solution to a problem or any individual thinking on her part must be all wrong, and she immediately proceeds to withdraw into herself. The result of this natural attitude, if not corrected, may develop into an unfortunate state of introspection which we know can become serious.

To Teach True Religious Life

Certainly it is the duty of a superior to give her subjects the correct idea of religious life. She must instruct her Sisters, speaking to them as women, not as children or grown-up little girls. It is her duty to explain to them how to form a holy and Christlike life. The problem that Sisters want a solution to is this: how can a religious, being human and living in the world, surrounded by worldly interests, and following, of necessity, worldly pursuits, be *wholly* and *entirely* united to God and His interests? A good superior will answer these questions and will try to make her subjects understand the beauty and the value of the religious life, lived as a whole. She will teach by example and by precept. A Sister must be taught early in her religious life that purity of intention and love of God will sanctify all her contacts with the world and that everything she does can contribute to that wholeness of dedication which alone can lead to holiness. It is the whole person that must be sanctified.

To be able to convey such fundamental ideas intelligently, a superior herself should be well informed on these matters and have a true theological understanding of religious life. To live, and *enjoy living* the religious life a Sister must learn to love that life "to the mature measure of the fullness of Christ."

To Share in Divine Authority

Since all authority comes from God, it follows, as St. Paul says, that those in authority share in the power of God Himself. The superior to whom God has entrusted part of His divine authority has not only the right, but also the duty, to counsel wisely and to correct kindly, when necessary, so that the spiritual life may be a happy life and be built on a solid foundation. A superior should also learn how to combine the *official* authority which comes from her office, and personal authority which stems from competence and personal holiness. Using both prudently she cannot help having a tremendous power and influence for good. Without looking for any thought of gratitude or appreciation, she will fulfill her sacred responsibility daily towards her subjects, always straight-forwardly, remembering that she does not govern from within as God does, but from without, as a tool in His hands.

In speaking of this authority (nothing less than part of God's almighty power), let us remember a sentence from the first of these talks, "She is not prudent who knows what should be done, yet fails to do it." The following example illustrates the lack of prudence on the part of the superior.

In a small town in Pennsylvania a group of Sisters staffed a parish high school. One of these, let us call her Sister Chrysostom, was very popular with the students and the parishioners. The superior noticed that every Sunday, except on Recollection Sunday, Mr. and Mrs. Black (let us call them) visited with Sister Chrysostom. After a month or so the superior spoke to the Sister, saying that she did not think it was good for her to see Mr. and Mrs. Black so constantly. Sister Chrysostom did not vary her conduct and seemed undisturbed by the correction. A second warning also failed to stop the visits. This continued for several months. Then, one Saturday morning, Sister Chrysostom told her superior that she would be leaving the community that afternoon. "You needn't bother to get me secular clothes," she said sweetly enough. "Mr. and Mrs. Black have already given me everything I need. I intend to live with them." The superior urged Sister to think this over and if she must leave to go to some other town.

As might be expected, Sister Chrysostom paid no attention. She continued to live right in the parish, going to Sunday Mass with the Blacks, teaching in the public high school. True enough, before many months passed, Mrs. Black moved out, divorce proceedings began, and Mr. Black went through a civil marriage ceremony with the former Sister Chrysostom — a complete debacle of spiritual life for at least two and perhaps all three.

Hindsight is so much clearer than foresight. We cannot judge the superior too harshly. Nevertheless, the fact remains that she had a duty, not only to warn Sister Chrysostom, but also to forbid her to see her friends every Sunday. If necessary she could have enlisted the provincial's authority as well. I do not say that this would have prevented the tragedy, but it might have fortified the Sister's tottering spirituality. This superior saw the danger and yet failed to act, and did not give her higher superiors a chance to act either.

When a superior, through cowardice, fails to tell the Sisters their faults, she must expect that someone else will take over her duty. We have all had the experience of seeing certain individuals in a house become self-appointed monitresses. Such religious watch over all the movements and actions of other particular individuals and scrutinize everything they do, in time and out of time. They even break in "where angels fear to tread"; no place is too personal or sacred for them to enter. For example, a certain young Sister was being so constantly corrected by a Sister other than her superior, that she had to seek help from a psychiatrist. After all, it is the superior who must assume the responsibility of correcting Sisters. She is charged with helping them to grow in holiness. If her duties are usurped by uninhibited persons, the superior herself may be the cause of this disorder. When a superior finds her proper place in the scheme of things, she is a real source of strength, helping her Sisters to actualize their spiritual life here and now.

To Foster the Spiritual Life

According to Father Corcoran, a local superior has not only the right but the duty to contribute all *she* has to the spiritual life of her subjects. To exercise this right and fulfill her duty a superior must strive to learn more and more about the spiritual life. She must learn all she can about the psychology of a soul and the theology necessary to guide that soul so that the individual may, as St. Teresa of Avila says, "advance according to the graces of light and interior spirit given her by God."

The superior of a house creates the atmosphere of religion, of love, of prayer, of confidence, of joy, of reverence, of humility and of holy fear. All these virtues are absolutely necessary requisites for a religious superior if her household is to enjoy charity and peace. Supposing a superior does not have these virtues, what can be done? How can she give what she does not have? If she is truly an interior soul she will recognize her need and she will pray. Grace will not be wanting if she asks for it. She must spare no effort, either by prayer or sacrifice, to establish the harmony just mentioned. If she, herself, creates an attitude of unanimity, she will establish such a religious spirit that all will live the rule lovingly.

From the moment one is appointed to the office of local superior she becomes an instrument, good or bad, in the hands of God to form the likeness of Christ in her subjects. God has high ambitions for religious souls and tries them as gold is tried in the fire. "I watched the Divine Goldsmith at His work as He stood by the furnace. Often He looked at the gold and put it back into the fire and then He said to me, 'It will at last be ready when I can see Myself therein.'" God looks for perfection in religious souls and it is the superior's duty to help in the process of perfecting her subjects. The sanctity of the apostolate will be no greater than the sanctity and personal virtues of each individual Sister who works in the apostolate.

The rule rightly applied to every situation as it affects each individual subject becomes for her a source of happiness. The superior must deal with each Sister as a person and as a whole person. In order to understand her as a person and help her to develop her potentialities the superior must recognize the individual differences in the religious and help her if she needs help, to discover what hidden riches she may possess and aid her to accomplish all that God expects from her because of her endowment.

The question of assigning Sisters to study for advanced degrees provides a good example here. What I have to say on this point is taken from my own observations and from what I have heard from priests and lay professors through the years. Sometimes Sisters are sent to universities to study in a certain field in which they have had no preliminary preparation. Moreover, these Sisters are expected to receive high grades in the classes they are taking and when they do not, the superiors do not treat them too kindly. One secular professor asked me one time if it were true that at the end of summer school the superiors assembled all the Sisters and read their grades for the summer aloud? I was surprised! I had never heard of this practice. Some Sisters had begged for higher grades because they said all the Sisters would hear their marks. Another secular professor asked me if it were true the Sisters were not given enough money for them to live as they should during the summer. Now, I can hardly believe this to be true.

We are told that mortification is the mainspring of fervor but I assure you that all the fervor in the world will not help a Sister through a difficult study program without something to cool off the fervor. The late Holy Father in his advice on renovation and adaptation said, "Imitate what your Holy Founder would do if he were living today, not what he would have done one hundred years ago." I am sure if my Holy Founder, Father Moreau, were living in Washington, D.C., he would approve of his religious having a few dollars in the summer for cokes.

All conditions should be made as favorable as possible for a Sister who is studying so that she will suffer no physical or mental harm from prolonged study. In fact, in our religious life we must pay attention to the individual differences of Sisters. Some get very little joy out of studying — it isn't as we like to have it — but it's a fact. They too must have some kind of recreational diversion. Sometimes these diversions are expensive, but again, we must use moderation in this as in everything else.

There are some useful hobbies that Sisters can develop — knitting, crocheting, gardening, stamp collecting, nursing African violets, or, as one Sister in Kansas did, accumulating a wide knowledge of Indian tribes, their history, customs, present status, etc. All these things are good when the subject is not permitted to run wild with them. The superior, herself, however, must keep her own hobbies in check.

For example, the superior of a lonely convent, situated in a district hostile to Catholics, had a passion for dogs. She told herself (and others) that the Sisters needed several good watchdogs to keep prowlers off. This was quite true and the provincial superior permitted the convent to have two dogs. Before long there were four dogs and eventually nine dogs were elbowing each other around in an effort to protect the Sisters. The Sisters themselves found that the convent was being run for the dogs. Puppies had a corner of the dormitory for their play pen. If the Sisters found their slippers chewed, their papers crumpled, their clothes scattered over the garden, they were told it was all their own fault for not keeping those things out of reach. Runways for the dogs were protected by fences and gates so that the Sisters had to walk the long way around. At recreation in the evening, each Sister had several dogs lying at her feet. The Sisters, feeling that no dog was worth arguing or quarreling about, nevertheless preserved a good spirit in the house. But the next General Chapter issued detailed instructions on the abuse of dogs in a convent.

Father Corcoran says also, "Whatever may be said for our basic similarities each one of us is an individual completely different and distinct from all others." It is this difference precisely which makes it possible for each of us to give God a distinctive kind of honor and praise. As creatures we are consecrated to that holy purpose. Each one of us is endowed with a soul and body of limited capacities. We are brought into the world at an express moment which God Himself has ultimately determined. We are given certain persons as our parents. Under their direction, we are formed and educated. Because of our origin, we are subject to this particular influence or that. As we grow, our individual temperament develops; consciously or unconsciously, we acquire a character. This absolutely unique individual gives to God a glory that is unique because our individual talents generate it. Whatever I have by nature or by acquisition must be directed to God's glory as *my* talent, *my* possibilities, and *my* potentialities, so developed and so consecrated.

As Dr. Goldbrunner repeats again and again in that remarkable little book, *Holiness Is Wholeness,* "We must live, each one, our own truth." It is our own individuality, which must be directed Godwards. In this sense he says, "There is no universal way of salvation. We have only the principles that must guide us." Superiors of religious must keep this truth constantly before their eyes.

This is a difficult situation. A superior may lay herself open to a charge of favoritism, because she does not exact the same of everyone. In this, she especially needs the guidance of the Holy Spirit. For instance, a Sister may be given permission to read detective stories. Well, her superior feels that she needs this distraction for one reason or another. A few years before or a few years later, this Sister perhaps would not have needed this type of diversion.

A young Sister of a well-known community went this summer to a week's musical institute given by a famous musician. With special permission, she and her companion stayed in the same house with the secular music teachers who attended. On the first morning, they slipped quietly out of the house and attended Mass at the local parish church. That evening, a woman came to them asking if she might accompany them to Mass. Of course, they said yes. She gave her name as Mary, just Mary.

The Sisters noticed that Mary always put on dark glasses when she entered the church and sat in a dark corner, although she faithfully followed her missal at Mass. On their last day, she told the Sisters her story. She had been twenty-two years in a large teaching order and had left only a few months before. She went to live with her brother in New Jersey but could not adjust herself to the secular atmosphere there. A kindly priest advised her to take a job as kitchen helper in this musician's summer camp. But Mary was aghast to find that the parish was staffed by the same order she had been in; indeed, she knew several of the Sisters there. Nevertheless, she persevered in going to daily Mass. She was miserably unhappy out in the world, had applied for re-entry, and was assured of a welcome back if the proper papers came through from Rome. "Why did you leave?" the Sisters asked. "I was teaching full time in school," said Mary. "Besides, I had fifty-four piano pupils. I became nervous and irritable. I slept as much as the others, but I must have needed more than they for I was always exhausted. When I asked to be relieved of some piano pupils, my superior said I was carrying no heavier a load than anyone else in that overworked house. Besides, we needed the money. In the end, I applied for a dispensation from my vows. Although the Mother General spoke very kindly to me and wanted me to stay with the community, promising a long rest period, still by that time I was obdurate. I insisted on leaving. Now I'm trying so hard to get back!" I wonder if the income from fifty-four music pupils was worth it.

To Help and Comfort

It is God's desire that superiors *help souls and comfort those* who need solace and ask for help. The old method of crushing souls in order to perfect them is outmoded. Many a Sister has gone to her grave misunderstood and misjudged by her superiors. When a Sister becomes what is called a "chronic complainer" she makes herself very unpopular with those who must watch over her. Every community knows religious who have suffered great humiliations through illness. Because the doctor could not find the malady, they were accused of pretending. Experience has often proved that these Sisters were really ill.

Of course, the other thing happens too; some Sisters are running to doctors constantly and have every new illness they read or hear about. Here is where the prudent superior will give them all the benefit of the doubt. A doctor, speaking to me not long ago about a problem he had with a certain Sister and her superior, said, "The superior was superficially kind and was not understanding. In the long run she would not prove to be sufficiently supportive."

But a Sister may need help in more than physical trials. Often a superior's kindly explanation may bring her safely over other crises. For instance, not long ago a young religious applied for admission to one of our outstanding universities. She built up great hopes and looked forward to the fine courses she would receive there. She told her friends that she was going to this university. Her application, after many weeks of processing, was finally rejected. The authorities gave no reason for refusal, but the intimation was that the Sister was a little too old to become a graduate student. She was thirty-six. This beautiful Sister, a religious one would be proud of, was heartbroken over this failure. When her superior asked her if she had ever met failure before, she had to acknowledge that she had not. This first failure was a shock. She was advised to put her hopes together again and to be grateful for the failure. In the whole world, with the exception of a few inflated egoists, probably no one has escaped the sense of failure at some time or other. This Sister, like all who meet failure for the first time, had forgotten for the moment that the importance of events is relative. Time gave her the opportunity to see that there is only one failure, to refuse to follow the will of God and not to see His providential workings in everyday circumstances of life.

To be of real help to her Sisters, to be able to distinguish between genuine need and the spurious complaints of those who want to be babied, a superior should establish a personal friendship with her subjects. When they are thoroughly at ease with her, and she with them, the real and the superficial become a little more apparent, although it is never easy to distinguish them entirely.

Holy Scripture is filled with examples of *inspiring personal relationships*. Let us recall the friendship of Christ with the little family at

Bethany. There was an understanding and a loving tie with them which He probably did not have with anyone else, even the Apostles during their ministry. Christ shared lovingly with Lazarus, Martha, and Mary all the virtues of His Divine personality and His irresistible charm.

The relationship between God and Job is another beautiful example of a personal friendship. Resting on the assurance of being understood, Job complained to God about all his misfortunes. God listened attentively and spoke to Job about the necessity of suffering, and how he should rejoice in being asked to suffer. Like Job, good religious should accept the Word of God as their food and encouragement and never be discouraged.

But I wonder how Job would have fared if he had spoken to some superiors as he spoke to God! If every Sister could be sure that superiors understood her as God understood Job, what a blessed community life we all would have.

Christ showed *no favoritism* in His dealings with souls. Everyone felt free to come to Him. St. Mary Magdalen, the sinner, and the woman taken in adultery were as dear to Him as was St. John, who probably never committed a serious sin in his life. If superiors wish to follow Christ and work out their relationships with their Sisters as He did, they will watch and wait for opportunities to give needed help, just as Christ waited for St. Paul on the desert trail. Superiors and subjects must strive to imitate Christ in their respect and love for each other. Such a friendship eliminates relations that are too personal and prompted by motives which are often mingled with questionable sentimentality. This is what we mean by relationships being whole and this is what we mean by their being holy.

Perhaps one can best illustrate the important part superiors play in forming the religious with whom they live by studying the story of the potter. The Lord directed Jeremias to go to the house of the potter and learn a lesson from him. "And I went down into the potter's house; and behold he was doing a work on the wheel. And the vessel was broken which he was making of clay with his hands; and turning he made another vessel, as it seemed good in his eyes to make it. Then the word of the Lord came to me saying, 'Cannot I do with you as this potter, O House of Israel?' saith the Lord. 'Behold as clay is in the hands of the potter, so are you in my hand, O House of Israel.'"

The story of the potter teaches a great lesson in relationship — no one works alone, but one is dependent upon the other. The clay out of which we are made is in the hands of the potter, our superior; the potter is in the hands of God. Sometimes the potter can form beautiful works in individual souls, depending on the cooperation of these individuals with divine grace. Some souls are able, with very little help from their superiors or from anyone, to reach a high degree of beauty by cooperating with God's grace. The weaker vessels, those that are left half-formed or broken into shapeless clay, need time and patience to bring out the potential beauty inherent in these broken fragments.

From all eternity God has ordained that the superior's duty is to pick up the pieces of the broken clay and form them into the pattern of Christ. Like the Divine Potter, she makes them into "another vessel as it seemed good in his eyes to make."

HIGHER SUPERIOR'S SUPPORT NEEDED

If superiors and subjects are ever going "to work together unto good" a third human influence must be working with them. This is the local superior's higher superior. Unless the superior is supported and her ideas are upheld, unless she can meet with her higher superiors on a common ground of sincerity and honest thinking, and unless she can express herself freely even when she may differ from her higher superior, she can accomplish nothing for the Sisters under her care. All her endeavors will be in vain. In order that the ideal set forth in this discussion be realized, there must be, then, on the human side, three persons, not two, who have definite roles to play — the subject, her superior, and the higher superior. For each, it is a challenging role. Under the guidance and inspiration of the Holy Spirit, a harmonious wholeness or togetherness of these three can result in that high holiness which the state of perfection promotes, and, through God's grace, can achieve.

CONCLUSION

One of the essential duties of a religious superior, therefore, is to use every means possible to draw out the inherent values, the potential virtues that lie hidden in her subjects. If she prays, God will give the superior the grace of office to accomplish great things for souls. He will give her the supernatural power to form beautiful vessels out of broken, shattered ones, provided she herself builds up her own spiritual life. She can do this only through a thorough understanding of that life, its rules, its constitutions, its spirit, and its purpose. Complete sacrifice of self is the necessary price that every superior must pay. Superiors must, above all, have a real Christlike love for each individual Sister so that everyone can say, "See how they love one another. How good it is for Sisters to dwell together in unity."

In conclusion I would like to leave with you a few thoughts which may serve as a guide through that maze — a superior's day. The religious superior for her own spiritual development should often reflect on the truth that prudence is the common trait of the saints: not only does one find prudence exemplified in the lives of martyrs and bishops; but also in the lives of virgins and confessors. The *Book of Proverbs* tells us . . . He best discerns who has knowledge of holy things. Let us turn then, to Her who above all others possesses this knowledge, the Virgin Most Prudent. To Her the Church has applied the words: Good Counsel is mine . . . discernment and high courage are my gifts (*Book of Proverbs* 8, 14).

VI

Personal Counsel by the Superior

God in His infinite wisdom sees the whole of His creation as the unfolding of a definite plan. In every age He raises up persons whose special gifts make them uniquely suited to the development of that part of the plan which is their immediate task. Thus, in our present social milieu, when the great mass of humanity is in many places reduced merely to tables of statistics, so many million to be fed, to be housed, to be educated, to be brought to the sacraments, those with the eyes of faith can see the providence of God in His selection of Pope John XXIII as His Vicar. By his own favorite characterization, our Holy Father is first of all a shepherd. And by Our Lord's own words, the shepherd sees his flock, not as an aggregate, but as individuals. Already the world has recognized the meekness, the humility, the generosity, and the personal concern with which the present Holy Father has begun his work in his own diocese of Rome, endeavoring to understand the problems of the parish priests, the people, the schools, the sick, the prisoners, so that he may give them the help they need and share with them the wise counsel of an ever-faithful Shepherd.

The virtues so well exemplified in the life of Pope John XXIII should serve as a pattern for every local superior. This personal concern of our Holy Father should be what each superior should endeavor to acquire in order to meet the needs of each Sister. Personal concern for the individual Sister is the very heart of the problem we wish to discuss in this paper. No matter how large or how small the institute in which a superior has been placed, her Sisters should be her first consideration and they should never become for her merely a matter of groups, of statistics, pigeon-holed into convenient categories. People differ very much from each other; what is good for one, may be bad for another. Sisters are people and even though they are living a sacrificial life they are still human and want to be treated as human beings. Each Sister is a unique personality, and if she is to grow in the image and likeness of Christ she must be treated as an integrated person. This discussion, therefore, is an attempt to present some new concepts and skills that might be helpful to the superior in establishing some constructive, stimulating relationships through the procedure of counseling. These ideas are not meant to supplant the worthwhile principles that Father Corcoran has so clearly explained to us. They merely give another light on the same subject. They are to serve as a possible means of increasing our desire to learn more about the subject of counseling so that we may become better superiors.

In order to understand the role of the superior as counselor, we must first consider her proper place among the three persons cooperating in this work; and second, the proper place of her counseling activities among her other duties. There are three persons in whom we are especially interested in the counseling situation. They are the superior, the priest, and the subject.

As Father Corcoran has reminded us, the Church in her wisdom has provided spiritual direction for all religious. Canon law is most explicit in safeguarding the privileges of the Sisters in this respect. And yet, from experience I know that superiors in attempting to help Sisters with their personal problems sometimes unconsciously take over the duties of a spiritual director. Those who have through experience learned the difference between the role of the superior and that of the priest will not intrude when subjects need help that only a priest can give. If the superior is aware that priestly counsel is needed or that it would contribute in any way to the spiritual growth of a Sister, it is her duty to do what she can to provide such counsel and at the same time to exercise the proper, prudent measure of regulatory supervision.

In the past ten years counseling as a science has made some remarkable strides; yet most of us are unaware of the values that lie inherent in the new procedures dealing with personal relationships. Science tells us that there is a big gap between how people actually think they can help others and how they might really help them if they understood better some of these modern techniques. It is my intention today to present a few of the findings which modern research has discovered and apply them to the superior's problem of counseling. This knowledge of modern research will, I hope, aid superiors to analyze some of their own difficulties and to correct any faulty procedure that they may have unconsciously developed during the years. It is to be desired that the success with which these tools have been used in other areas will encourage superiors to explore and accept them where they can be of assistance in the field of counseling in religious life. At this time I am reminded of the good advice given by a Benedictine monk to his religious family. "The less a monk thinks of converting the world and the more he thinks of converting himself, the sooner the world will be converted." Our own methods of dealing with Sisters through no fault of ours may be so awkward that unless we correct ourselves and learn some new procedures we cannot hope to reach souls in the way we must reach them.

With respect to the superior's counseling activities which are proper to her office, it will be helpful in the beginning to distinguish "counseling" from guidance and other superior-subject relationships which contribute to spiritual and intellectual growth. This is not to imply that in daily living there will be a sharp separation of these activities from one another, or that counseling as a separate function can be looked upon as an independent tool in the formation of the religious life, or that all relationships are counseling situations. Religious formation is an integrating process, using many tools and adapting them always to the ability and to the special needs and interests of each Sister. Nevertheless, the more clearly we understand the art of counseling, the more we shall become aware of the opportunities for using it, and, with God's help, the greater will be the success we may hope to attain. Father William C. Bier, S.J., writing in the February, 1959, issue of *Pastoral Psychology,* distinguishes counseling from guidance and from psychotherapy.

In his article, "Goals in Pastoral Counseling," Father states that guidance is a form of education. It terminates frequently in information, advice, and changes in behavior. It is the responsibility of the person giving guidance to see that the information imparted is accurate and that it is appropriate to the individual being advised. He says that much guidance is done in novitiates and houses of study. Any local superior is expected to give her subjects guidance in the work of the institute for which her foundation is responsible.

Psychotherapy derives from psychiatry. Its sphere is that of mental disturbance or the solving of problems involving unconscious attitudes that are emotional and not *properly* related to reality. Counseling deals with this phase of behavior only insofar as it gives an indication of the necessity of counseling. That which properly deserves the name of counseling is based on the science of psychology. It emphasizes understanding the person rather than the imparting of information. This also includes self-understanding on the part of the counselee. It is therefore not synonymous with advising or with psychotherapy. The key to progress in counseling comes through the self-activity of the individual which the counselor makes possible. The counselee through this self-activity or "thinking aloud" is able to free herself from present difficulties and to make her own future decisions. It is the thinking done while in conference with the counselor that produces this freedom of expression.

At this point it should be noted in what the *sine qua non* for ideal counseling consists. We have learned from the scholarly opinions of Rev. Charles A. Curran that there must be a complete giving of self both on the part of the counselor and the counselee if the counseling process is to bear fruit. It must be a true giving of two individual selves. And here, I quote from Father Curran: "This is what constitutes a relationship of *both loving* and *being loved*. But obviously this is not love in the popular, emotional sense. Rather, it seems to approximate that high kind of spiritual love which the ancients called *amor benevolentiae,* a love that gives of itself entirely and seeks no return from the other except the other's best fulfillment of himself." This is a respectful dignified love of others, not merely a matter primarily of feeling. This selfless giving must then be on such a high spiritual plane that only the more perfect well-being and greater good of each other is sought.

Rev. Albert Grau, S.J., another authority on the subject of counseling, says that there are three major elements that one must consider in the counseling process. They are the counselee, the counselor, and the interview. Furthermore, in considering the counselee, in this case the Sister, we must look at her from three different angles: (1) the way she thinks she is; (2) the way she would like to be; (3) the way she actually is.

As we said before, the counselor, who in this discussion is the superior, must always work on the principle that the Sister alone is responsible for whatever adjustment is to be brought about in herself. The superior must believe that when a Sister uses all the God-given helps, both natural and supernatural, that she possesses, "she has within herself the power to become psychologically mature and properly self-directive." Whether or not the Sister will realize her power to achieve this complete development depends on many factors. However, the superior must give her the opportunity to use this power and permit her to express herself by words or silence in whatever manner she wishes without fear of reprisal for using her freedom of expression. For the ideal interview, then, the superior must take every opportunity to acquire first, a deeper knowledge of the Sister she is counseling; second, a clear appreciation of the Sister's problems; and third, if possible, a mastery of technique that will enable her to help the Sister make progress toward resolving her own problem.

As I see it, the whole idea of counseling in religious life is to help some particular Sister achieve through her own efforts a purposeful planning of life through a process that will be functional. The superior's understanding and friendly attitude must be such that good rapport will be brought about in every situation so that in time the Sister will be convinced that she is loved, understood, and capable of solving her own problems.

What is there that we can learn from methods of counseling in its present stage of development that will help superiors to awaken in a subject an awareness of her difficulties and through clinical counseling aid her to help herself? Most of us here today are not professionally-trained psychologists. And yet counseling, as I have suggested, is a clinical, scientific, psychological procedure. However, the counseling interview when properly so called has a technique which with a little practice can be learned. While we all know many hidden miracles in which God's grace has effected great and good things by means of poorly fashioned instruments, we realize, too, that He expects us to learn and use to the best of our ability the knowledge that will enable us to fulfill our duties more perfectly. Whatever we can learn from science, study, the experience of others, or our own past experience is most desirable and should be profitable. Professional help for superiors in the techniques of counseling may be learned within the limits of a workshop, such as was conducted for the clergy this summer at the Catholic University. If priests find the need of special classes in counseling so should religious superiors. I say that all these helps are good and that we should use every means available to make ourselves more helpful to others; but in all this there is a fact we must never lose sight of — a power that is more valuable than all others — we must have great confidence in God and in His grace, and so much distrust of ourselves that no matter what natural helps we may be able to acquire, we are absolutely dependent for all counseling on the inspiration of the Holy Spirit.

Again returning to the methods applied in clinical psychology, we find that there are certain ones which we may very well adopt. Their purpose is to assist the counselor to achieve a more "stable, mature, and reasonable way of life." The three following principles point the way in which these resources can be used effectively. The first may be stated as follows: "Think of the Sister as a person and not as a problem or a case. Use what you may have learned concerning general types; you may even know which type this Sister is, but do not so characterize her. Look for the special traits that highlight her individuality; they may be an important clue. She is one particular lamb needing help; not one-twentieth of your flock."

It happens with all of us that we find certain Sisters easier to deal with than others; but the "others" are the superior's responsibility also and often need more encouragement and help than the ones who are easy to get along with. I recall a Sister who was always classified as a "problem." When I was a young Sister I did not know what this expression meant since the persons with whom I lived always seemed to love one another and as far as I knew there were no problems. In later years I learned from the Sister herself why she was considered a problem. She knew that everyone labeled her as such. When I first met her she greeted me with "This is your problem child." During the interview that followed Sister revealed to me many things that at that time surprised me very much. After Sister left, I was so disturbed that it took me a long time to get over what had been told me, if I ever did. The two concerned in this story are in heaven, I hope, so I am free to tell you about them. This so-called problem child had a very sensitive nature and felt things keenly. Her home life had not been a very happy one. She never spoke of her family. It happened that in her younger days she had a great admiration for her local superior. She confided in her and told her all the hidden sorrows of her past life in order to relieve her mind. She hoped that by this means she could attain peace of soul and begin her religious life over again in a more joyful spirit. Her superior seemed to be always most understanding and sympathetic and proved helpful to this Sister on many occasions through the years.

For some reason or other, after a while the superior withdrew her interest from this young Sister and later imprudently revealed the Sister's confidences, not as one might suppose to a member of her own community (which unfortunately happens sometimes), but to a secular friend of the Sister who also repeated the confidence. Consequently this young Sister withdrew into herself, became introspective and spent most of her time in her room when not teaching. She was never sociable at table or in recreation, and seldom enjoyed friendly conversation with anyone. Here was a potentially good Sister who became a "problem" through the imprudence and injustice of a counselor.

On the basis of what is known about modern research how would one treat this particular Sister? Even though the Sister felt justified in her long established attitude of aloofness, what procedure could be used to lead her to convince herself that she is no longer a "problem"? What means should one take to have her come to the realization through her own efforts that she is a person and must be respected as such? Modern psychology, as I mentioned before, would have us look for the special traits that highlight this Sister's individuality; they may be an important clue in helping to counsel her.

The second principle of clinical research states that the role of the counselor is predominately that of the listener. She must permit the Sister to solve her own problems in her own frame of reference, she must reserve her own judgment and make no decisions; she must seemingly not try to find out what is at "the heart of the matter." The superior should therefore choose her questions carefully and inject them only when it is necessary to initiate a line of thinking or redirect a line which promises to be fruitless. Many times all that a Sister needs is an opportunity to express herself to a really interested and affectionately sympathetic listener. The actual verbalizing of her thought may throw such light on their meaning that she will see for herself the nature of her own difficulty and will be able to judge and evaluate it, and even to solve it herself. If, on the other hand, the counselee must continually redirect her thinking to adjust to the superior's frequent and perhaps poorly chosen questions, many valuable outcomes will be lost.

A superior of a missionary community told me not long ago about a Sister who was carrying a heavy cross but who would not reveal the cause to anyone in the community. Her superior made every effort to be particularly kind to this Sister hoping that eventually she would feel free enough to tell her what was worrying her so she could be of some definite help. One day the Sister was passing the superior's office and stopped at the door to say something. Immediately the superior arose from her desk, invited the Sister into the office, and she herself took a seat not behind her desk where she usually sat, but in front of it, making the situation informal and putting the Sister at ease. After a few minutes, the Sister began to talk. She remained with her superior one hour. During this time all that the superior did was to listen. After the interview was over, the Sister thanked her superior for all the help she had given her and said, "I had no intention when I came in here of telling you anything. Now I know what I must do and with God's grace I shall do it. You have helped me very much." This method of just listening is one of the simplest of counseling techniques. The superior in this case had to have great patience and perseverance and make every effort not to interrupt the Sister's flow of thought. Had she injected her own ideas, the interview would have been a failure. The superior deserved much credit, too, for by her kindly sympathetic manner, she created a good rapport.

The third of these clinical principles urges the counselor to think of the counselee as a person who is in the process of *becoming*. She is not to be looked upon as a pattern fixed and determined but as a person capable of growth and development; therefore, neither the superior nor the Sister being counseled should be bound by the Sister's past attitudes and conduct. If the superior makes it evident to the counselee that she is thinking of her as one capable of reaching perfection, she will have prepared the ground for a desire on the part of a Sister to realize her potentialities. In her own heart, the superior must conceive the Sister as one capable of creative inward development.

In order to avail ourselves of all the opportunities that will help us to acquire skill in counseling let us ask the advice of our Sister and priest psychologists in drawing up suggestions for the initial counseling interview, for subsequent interviews to create a better understanding and rapport, for signs which may indicate that the counselee now understands herself and her place in God's plan and is ready to meet future contingencies by making her own wise decisions. Let us ask professional assistance, also, in compiling an annotated book-list on counseling, suited to various degrees of scholastic preparation in this field. And let us ask for the organization of a workshop in which the emphasis shall be less on the necessity of superior-subject counseling and the virtues and characteristics of the good superior counselor, necessary though these surely are, and more on professional concepts and techniques. In the former areas, with God's grace and great good will, much self-help is possible; but in the latter, that is, professional aid, many of us have had little or no experience.

It may be countered that in this discussion of counseling there is nothing new; that superior-subject counseling has been with us since the origin of religious orders; that we are merely putting a new look on a technique that dates back to the beginning of religious orders. True, every community has a rule on Direction, or its equivalent, and this rule has been helpful to superiors in directing Sisters for centuries. As St. Francis de Sales says, many souls have obtained salvation by means of direction. Counseling, however, is not just a new look on direction; it is something really new. It is a development that is the result of modern scientific psychology. In the formation of religious, we cannot afford to ignore any field of research that might help some Sister to accomplish greater things for her own soul and for the souls of others. We must learn every new device that is good and share our knowledge with others.

In what way might this sharing of our experiences prove helpful? It would not surprise me if the Sisters in need of experienced counseling would fall into a few general types; and these few types would be common to most religious communities. While I am not retreating from my position that the essential characteristic of superior-subject counseling must be its acceptance of a Sister as an individual and not as a type, still I think that it would be useful for us to review some of these general types. I submit the following with a feeling of assurance that they will be familiar to all.

The first deals with the Sister who has few or no difficulties. She keeps her rule, loves her religious life, prays well, and seems to get along with everyone. She likes to be noticed a little, though, and makes occasions to visit the superior's office frequently for trifling permissions. She is the first to answer the superior's call. She never disturbs the peace of the house. She could be a busy-body, and although a very nice busy-body, she will never reach the degree of maturity which makes for sanctity. She is not the type out of which saints are made. The second type is the Sister who is constantly against the government. She always has a problem which no one is capable of solving. She complains that her superior pays no attention to her, that she wants only the young Sisters around. She shows a bad spirit at the table, at recreation, and never seems to understand that she might sometimes be wrong.

The third type is the Sister who is really worried and with cause. She needs help. Because of past experiences she does not wish to take her troubles to the superior. She has heard from other Sisters that this particular superior does not keep confidences. She feels a certain resentment which develops into a hostility toward all superiors. She feels that she cannot trust anyone.

Now these three types are considered normal. Such Sisters teach their classes, attend religious exercises, and present themselves on retreat Sunday for direction. What shall a superior do to help these Sisters? How can she use the techniques of counseling to help them to understand their problems and the causes of these problems both in themselves and in their surroundings? It is of little use for the superior to give her analysis of the problem and extract from the Sister a promise to try to look at things differently. Progress will come only when the Sister is led by prudent questioning to discover the problem for herself, when the rapport achieved in the counseling situation is so perfect that she feels the strength of the counselor's desire to help her and is encouraged to face the conclusions to which the understanding of her difficulties must inevitably lead. Any superior would want to achieve this. But when one is dealing with so complex a thing as the human mind, good will is not enough. The superior must go out of her way to make this rapport possible.

Every superior also needs a certain knowledge of counseling skills. She will then be prepared to render greater help to those who need it. All these viewpoints on counseling which we have considered are important. But before concluding this talk I should like to place before you an ideal that not only includes all that has been said so far but also places emphasis on the ultimate objective that the counselor should have in mind. In all her counseling activities her purpose should be to inspire every Sister by precept and by example to live not merely in her own little personal world, but to spread her wings — even as modern science has taught her to do — and to soar beyond the limited boundaries of self into that universe of unlimited space and time that we have long known and understood as the Mystical Body of Christ.

The contemporary world in which we live almost forces upon us the reality of this doctrine. As our boundaries of knowledge have expanded, so must our love and service reach out to other selves. Space travel and modern means of communication and transportation are bringing other worlds so close to us that just considering this fact from the natural standpoint we are convinced that it will be a part of wisdom, if we wish to survive, to live not by competition or isolation but by charity and union with one another. Thus the discoveries of modern science point to the fact that our ideal is to live not merely by desire and word, but by action — the doctrine of the Mystical Body of Christ. The expansion of our physical boundaries is making us realize the responsibilities that accompany this gathering together of all human beings. We know, as religious, that we are bound together not only by the ties of our human nature, but also by those bonds which unite us to the family of God. This union is the basis of that living charity that should motivate all our activities.

If a superior gives to her subjects this total view; if she stresses the ideal of seeing Christ in all souls; if she leads the person to forget self in serving others, then she will have helped the Sister she counsels to attain that true integrated personality which leads to Christian perfection.

BIBLIOGRAPHY

Father James, O.F.M. Cap., *The Spirit of Christ*. Westminister, Md.; Newman, 1946.

Bruno M. Hagspiel, S.V.D., *Convent Readings and Reflections*. Milwaukee, Wisconsin; Bruce, 1959.

Ignaz Watterott, O.M.I., *Guidance of Religious* (tr. Simon), St. Louis, Mo.; Herder, 1952.

Josef Goldbrunner, *Holiness in Wholeness* (tr. Goodman), New York, N.Y.; Pantheon Books, 1955.

Dom Basil Hemphill, O.S.B.; *The Joy of Serving God*, St. Louis, Mo.; Herder, 1948.

Felix D. Duffy, C.S.C., *Manual for Novices*, St. Louis, Mo.; Herder, 1957.

Very Rev. Adolph Tanquerey, *Doctrine and Devotion* (tr. Arand), Tournai, Belgium, Desclee and Co., 1933.

Abbot Gasquet and Canon Mackey, O.S.B., (translators), *The Spiritual Conferences of St. Francis de Sales.* Westminster, Md.; Newman, 1943.

Johannes Lindworsky, S.J., *The Psychology of Asceticism* (tr. Heiring) Baltimore, Md.; Carroll Press, 1950.

Louis Colin, C.S.S.R., *The Practice of the Rule* (tr. Heinmann), Westminster, Md., Newman, 1957.

Proceedings of the 1958 Sisters' Institute of Spirituality; Notre Dame, Indiana; Notre Dame Press, 1959.

Gerald Kelly, S.J., *Guidance for Religious,* Westminster, Md.; Newman, 1957.

Charles E. Sheedy, C.S.C., *The Christian Virtues,* Notre Dame, Indiana; Notre Dame Press, 1949.

Willibald Demal, O.S.B., D.D., *Pastoral Psychology in Practice* (tr. Conway) New York, N.Y.; Kenedy, 1955.

Obedience. Religious Life Series III. Westminster, Md., Newman, 1953.

Planning for the Formation of Sisters. Proceedings of the Sisters Formation Conferences, 1956-57, New York, N.Y.; Fordham U. Press, 1958.

Sister Formation Bulletin, Vol. I, No. 1 — Vol. IV, No. 4; Milwaukee, Wis.; Marquette U. Press, 1959.

Poverty. (tr. Sheppard), Religious Life Series IV, Westminster, Md.; Newman, 1954.

Communal Life. Religious Life Series VIII, Westminster, Md.; Newman, 1957.